The Minoans and Mycenaeans: The History of the Developed Ancient Greek Cultures

By Charles River Editors

Minoan art

About Charles River Editors

Charles River Editors is a boutique digital publishing company, specializing in bringing history back to life with educational and engaging books on a wide range of topics. Keep up to date with our new and free offerings with this 5 second sign up on our weekly mailing list, and visit Our Kindle Author Page to see other recently published Kindle titles.

We make these books for you and always want to know our readers' opinions, so we encourage you to leave reviews and look forward to publishing new and exciting titles each week.

Introduction

A fresco depicting a Mycenaean woman

Nearly 2,500 years after the Golden Age of Athens, people across the world today continue to be fascinated by the Ancient Greeks. But who did the Ancient Greeks look up to? The answer to that question can be found in Homer's *The Odyssey*, in which Odysseus makes note of "a great town there, Cnossus, where Minos reigned." It was perhaps the earliest reference to the Minoan civilization, a mysterious ancient civilization that historians and archaeologists still puzzle over, but a civilization that renowned historian Will Durant described as "the first link in the European chain."

Nearly 2,000 years before Homer wrote his epic poems, the Minoan civilization was centered on the island of Crete, a location that required the Minoans to be a regional sea power. And indeed they were, stretching across the Aegean Sea from about 2700-1500 BCE with trade routes extending all the way to Egypt.

The Minoans may have been the first link in the "European chain", leading to the Ancient Greeks and beyond, but questions persist over the origins of the civilization, the end of the civilization, and substantial parts of their history inbetween, including their religion and buildings.

In the wake of the Minoans, a Greek culture flourished and spread its tentacles throughout the western Mediterranean region via trade and warfare. Scholars have termed this pre-Classical Greek culture the Mycenaean culture, which existed from about 2000-1200 BCE, when Greece, along with much of the eastern Mediterranean, was thrust into a centuries long dark age. However, before the Mycenaean culture collapsed, it was a vital part of the late Bronze Age Mediterranean system and stood on equal footing with some of the great powers of the region, such as the Egyptians and Hittites.

Despite being ethnic Greeks and speaking a language that was the direct predecessor of classical Greek, the Mycenaeans had more in common with their neighbors from the island of Crete, who are known today as the Minoans. Due to their cultural affinities with the Minoans and the fact that they conquered Crete yet still carried on many Minoan traditions, the Mycenaeans are viewed by some scholars as the later torchbearers of a greater Aegean civilization, much the way the Romans carried on Hellenic civilization after the Greeks.

Given that the Mycenaeans played such a vital role on the history in the late Bronze Age, it would be natural to assume there are countless studies and accurate chronologies on the subject, but the opposite is true. Although the Mycenaeans were literate, the corpus of written texts from the period is minimal, so modern scholars are left to use a variety of methods in order to reconstruct a proper history of Mycenaean culture.

In fact, even the name "Mycenaean" can be a bit misleading since it refers only to one locale in Greece. However, since the city was the first Bronze Age site discovered, it became a reference point for archeologists and historians to use to refer to any Bronze Age discoveries in Greece. Archeology provides the base for any study of the ancient Mycenaeans; since many of their cities were replaced and built over in classical, medieval, and modern times, excavations of the Bronze Age cities can tell modern scholars how these people lived and died. Closely related to archaeology is art history, which can be the study of any material culture including pottery, sculptures, reliefs, and jewelry. The Homeric epics also provide some information about Mycenaean culture, though Homer was a poet who lived hundreds of years after the collapse of the Mycenaean culture. Classical Greek historians and geographers also wrote about the Mycenaeans, but their works should be consulted with caution as some of their statements have proved false and they, like Homer, received much of their information through oral traditions. Finally, the few extant Mycenaean written documents can help tell modern scholars what the Mycenaeans found most important in life. When all of the sources are consulted, they reveal that the Mycenaean culture was as vibrant as any other during the Bronze Age.

The Minoans and Mycenaeans: The History of the Civilizations that First Developed Ancient Greek Culture shines a light on these influential groups, providing a comprehensive overview of their reigns and their lasting influence on European art, culture, trade, and more. Along with pictures depicting important people, places, and events, you will learn about the Minoans and Mycenaeans like never before.

Minoan vase, circa 1500 BCE

The Minoans and Mycenaeans: The History of the Civilizations that First Developed Ancient Greek Culture

About Charles River Editors

The Discovery of a Bronze Age Culture in Greece

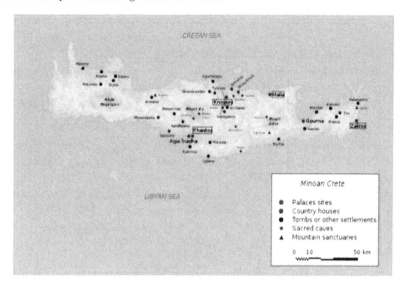

Major Minoan Sites Map: Bibi Saint-Pol

In the 2,000 years after the decline of the Ancient Greeks, the West was still obsessed with discovering anything related to antiquity that they could, culminating with the discovery of the city of Troy by Heinrich Schliemann in the 1870s. Still, until the end of the 19th century, interest far outpaced findings. Until the 20th century, ideas concerning pre-classical Greece consisted of a few sketchy and wild speculations based on a smattering of looted artworks that appeared on the market. This changed abruptly with the remarkable discoveries of hitherto unknown rich Greek Bronze Age cultures by Schliemann, Arthur Evans and others.

Schliemann

The larger-than-life, amateur archaeologist, Schliemann, was a wealthy industrialist who in his early retirement used his fortune to pursue his belief that the city of Troy, known through Homer's epic poems, was an actual historical place and not, as was commonly believed, a mythical city. Beginning in 1871, at Hisarlik in Turkey, he excavated a large metropolis which he concluded was Homer's Troy. Schliemann published the astonishing results of his excavation *Troja und seine Ruinen (Troy and Its Ruins)* in 1875. He further expanded the knowledge of pre-Classical culture in Greece with excavations, begun in 1876, at Mycenae.

Schliemann will forever be remembered for finding the city associated with the Trojan War and Homer's Iliad, but his findings at Troy were consequential for what it told researchers about the Bronze Age, in the centuries before the Trojan War was presumably fought. In pursuit of further evidence of Greek Bronze Age culture, Schliemann continued to work at Troy, partnered in a dig at Tiryns, and opened up a few trenches at Knossos on the island of Crete. He was prevented from continuing his work at Knossos by inability to acquire the site.

In 1899 the British gentleman scholar, Arthur Evans, acquired a small area of the site at Knossos and began the process of uncovering what turned out to be an extensive Bronze Age city. His excavations continued until 1914, were resumed after the First World War, and continued until 1932. By 1906 Evans had sufficient archeological information to publish a chronology of the Bronze Age culture he discovered at Knossos, which he called Minoan. The name has stuck ever since.

Statue of Evans at the Palace of Knossos

What the people who built Knossos called themselves is still unknown. In Egypt, dating from the period of the rule of Queen Hatshepshut, 1590 - 1550 BCE, there are tomb paintings that show a delegation of individuals presenting tribute, and the individuals are dressed in costumes identical to those seen in the art unearthed at Knossos. Unfortunately, the surviving bits of the image do not name the tribute bearers, although later Egyptian tomb texts refer to a group of people "coming from the shores of Keftiu", a reference to part of Ancient Egypt. Thus, there are no certain links identifying the Keftiu with the people who built the city of Knossos on Crete, Evans's naming of the Minoans has been universally accepted as appropriate, even though it will never accurately explain who the Minoans were.

Before Evans published a detailed description of the excavations at Knossos, books intended for a general audience appeared describing the newly discovered Bronze Age Mycenaean and Minoan cultures of Greece. The entirely new picture of pre-Classical Greece with highly advanced architecture and art intrigued readers who were well acquainted with classical Greek art in museums in Europe and America.

Sir Arthur Evans by William Blake Richmond Photo: Marin Beek

In 1909, Evans published the first volume of his *Scripta Minoa: The Written Documents of*

Minoan Crete, in which he recorded the texts of inscribed tablets he had discovered at Knossos. In 1921 the first volume of his dig report, *The Palace of Minos*, appeared, and it was followed by four other volumes.

While Evans was concentrating on the rich site of Knossos, other archaeologists were contributing to the quickly expanding knowledge of the now named Minoan civilization. In 1900, German scholar Frederico Halbherr began digging at Phaistos in Crete, eventually uncovering a large Minoan city. Meanwhile, French archaeologist Pierre Demargne worked at a site near Mallia in Crete and in 1901 American Harriet Boyd Hawes began excavating the Minoan city of Gournia, about 40 miles east of Knossos. Hawes brought the exciting discoveries in Crete to the attention of the general public in 1922 in a book she co-authored with husband C.H. Hawes, entitled *Crete, the Forerunner of Greece*. The descriptions in these publications of a civilization which had previously been accessible only to specialists generated worldwide interest and created a new audience for the spectacular discoveries in Crete.

The fascination of the public in Minoan civilization, demonstrated by the throngs of tourists that began to tramp through the several archaeological sites on Crete and through the Heraklion Archaeological Museum, is in large measure a product of two novels by the English writer Mary Renault. As an undergraduate student, Renault became enthralled by the newly discovered civilization revealed by the digs at Knossos while lodging at Oxford University with her relative Arthur Evans, Keeper of the Ashmolean Museum. She put his scholarly stamp on her extraordinarily popular books, *The King Must Die* (1948) and *The Bull from the Sea* (1969), still widely available in print today.

Renault

The designation of Bronze Age culture in Crete as Minoan was a creation of Arthur Evans. He called the major building he uncovered at Knossos a palace. This palace he identified with King Minos, who was mentioned by Homer in the *Iliad* and *Odyssey*. Homer also says that the craftsman/architect Daedalus constructed a dancing floor or labyrinth on Crete in which the Minotaur, part man part bull, lived. In one of the Greeks' most famous myths, the hero Theseus was challenged to kill the Minotaur. He entered the Labrynth trailing a thread, as he has been told to do by Ariadne, daughter of King Minos and his wife Pasiphaë. Theseus penetrated the labyrinth to the Minotaur's lair, killed him and then followed the thread to escape the architectural trap. The story became expanded in subsequent versions; in Ovid's *Metamorphoses*, Daedalus builds an incredibly complex structure in which King Minos places his wife's son, the Minotaur. The beast was fathered by a white bull that the god Poseidon made the object of Pasiphaë's lust. Fittingly, the Minoans at Knosssos built a palace of such complexity that its structure has been characterized by the adjective labyrinthine.

Ruins of the palace at Knossos

The Chronology of Minoan Civilization

Regardless of whether the naming of the Minoan civilization was accurate or appropriate, Arthur Evans did establish a working chronology of the various levels of Minoan remains at Knossos, identifying Early, Middle and Late Minoan periods. Evans also divided each of these periods into three sub-periods, and in later adjustments to his chronology, the sequence of Minoan civilization has been identified as it is related to the major municipal structure, the palace.

However, not all historians and archaeologists agreed that the large and complex buildings found at many Minoan sites are indeed palaces, so different archaeologists and writers apply different names to the periods in the chronology. Moreover, given that the civilization existed over 4,500 years ago, it should not be surprising that the dates in the following chronology are not firmly fixed, and, as the archaeology of Minoan sites continues, refinements are made to the description of the evolution of Minoan art and architecture. Finally, as with all arbitrary chronologies of ancient and indeed of modern civilizations, it is important to keep in mind that the spread of the Minoans and their existence over the course of a millennium meant their culture did not evolve in a uniform fashion, even though the civilization is all referred to by one name.

In what has been called the Prepalatial Period by some and Early Minoan by others (3000-2000 BCE) the first signs of a post Neolithic Culture or Bronze Age appear in a number of excavated houses. How this culture evolved is unknown. There are at Knossos several levels of Neolithic remains that point to as much as a 3000 year pre-Minoan occupation of the site. The development of ability to create bronze implements not only took considerable time but required the mineral resources of copper and tin that if not found locally could be imported.

In the **Protopalatial Period** or Early Middle Minoan Period, the old palaces at Knossos, Phaistos and Mallia were constructed, but they were destroyed by an earthquake around 1700 BCE It has been hypothesized by some that after this disaster a people called the Luvians, from south west Anatolia, settled in Crete and brought with them their written language, with a script that has been said to be similar to Linear A, the name given to the first Minoan writing.

The Protopalatial Period was followed by the **Neopalatial Period** or Late Middle Minoan Period (1700-1600 BCE). The name of the era comes from the fact that new palaces were begun at Knossos and Phaistos. The finest of Minoan decorative art and the finest frescoes in the palaces come from this period. Such was the flourishing of Minoan civilization in this era that some have supposed that Crete became overpopulated.

Fresco at the Palace of Knossos

Like their predecessors, these second palatial structures appear to have been destroyed by earthquake and in some cases consequent fires at the end of this period. The coastal cities of Crete, the harbours and trading centers, were also destroyed.

In the **Late Minoan Period** (1600-1400 BCE), the Palace at Knossos was partially rebuilt. It is possible that the Mycenaeans from mainland Greece attacked and possibly occupied Knossos, which was then in a very weakened state. Around 1375 BCE, the final palace at Knossos and other palaces in Crete were destroyed by some unknown catastrophe, perhaps more earthquakes or by an invasion of Dorians, the founders of what we know as ancient Greek culture.

The Palace Culture of the Minoans

As with any ancient civilization, one of the first things archaeologists and historians note are the defensive surroundings of the civilization's cities and settlements, which helps inform whether the civilization was constantly engaged in fighting outsiders or even each other. For example, defensive fortifications were found in some Mayan cities but not others, suggesting different experiences even within the same culture.

Despite being a maritime power that stretched across the Greek islands and traded as far away as Egypt, Minoan cities on Crete lacked defensive fortifications, which might suggest they lived in peace. However, given the experience of contemporaneous societies across the Mediterannean, and the spread of the Minoans themselves, this strikes historians as unlikely. Instead, the absence of trenches, walls and parapets surrounding the urban centers suggests that the Minoans were confident of their dominance in the region. Moreover, it indicates that the various cities on the island of Crete did not compete with each other in a way that led to armed aggression or civil war.

Still, in spite of this evidence, it is clear the Minoans were not entirely peaceful. Numerous depictions of men in armour and wielding swords plus ample pictorial evidence of the construction and use of shields are sufficient to show that the Minoans were capable of defending their power and commercial interests.

Minoan fresco of children boxing with each other

As the pioneer of Minoan archaeology, Arthur Evans was faced with the problem of naming the structures he unearthed at Knossos. Most names were, of course, based on the assumed function of the particular structure or room. In the absence of decipherable written records, and influenced by the well known story of the mythic King Minos of Knossos, whose name Evans used to label the Bronze Age culture he discovered there, Evans concluded that the huge structure at Knossos was a Palace. Like anyone else, Evans and the archaeologists who followed him brought to their work prejudices common to the world they inhabited. Evans, being a child of Victorian Britain brought up in a world of empire and regal munificence, and a gentleman in a society with a sophisticated class structure, determined that the richly decorated complex at Knossos could be nothing other than a royal palace. With this idea firmly fixed in his mind, he determined that the palace necessarily included such amenities as a Throne Room and the Queen's Apartments.

Since Evans' time many archaeologists have debated the merits of his nomenclature. There is a strong contingent among modern scholars that believe the designation of the large structure in Minoan cities is itself incorrect. They propose that there is sufficient evidence to conclude that the buildings at Zakros, Phaistos, Mallia and Knossos are not palaces but rather complexes that had an exclusively religious function in Minoan society. Some have even gone so far as to propose that the palace was necropolis or a huge burial site where the dead were tended by a large number of "priests" who lived in the so-called palace and performed public and private rituals there. In spite of the great probability that Minoan palaces were not really Bronze Age equivalents of the regal homes of Europe that we associate with the term palace, the use of the word by Evans has stuck, and it continues to be accepted with reservations as a simple generic term for the large Minoan structures.

The notion that the large central structures of Minoan cities exclusively served as a royal residence or religious sanctuary (monastery) is perhaps better replaced by considering them as a kind of multi-purpose community center. Modern archaeologists have found evidence that these palaces included artisans' workshops, storage vaults for trade goods and food, repositories of written documents (tablets), and places for the veneration of goddesses and gods and the performance of sacred rituals, including bull leaping and bathing.

In four of the Minoan cities that have been excavated on Crete, the largest structure dominating the community was what has been identified as a palace. Although earthquakes sporadically destroyed the Minoans' palaces, the palaces were rebuilt after their destruction, indicating their importance in the civic life of the Minoans.

The smallest of the palace-dominated cities in Crete is the palace at Zakros, and even that structure spanned about 25,000 square feet. Surrounding a central court that was about 90 feet by 40 feet were 150 rooms of varying sizes and functions. To the north of the court were store rooms and to the south was the Hall of Ceremonies. The ritual objects found in this room included rhytons or vessels for liquids (probably olive oil or wine) that were poured on altars to honor the gods. It has been suggested that these several vessels came from a storeroom on the second story that collapsed into the Hall itself.

Ruins of the Palace of Zakros

It is believed that what have been called the Royal Apartments occupied a range on the west side of the central court. Near them were found an archive with inscribed tablets, a treasury with luxury objects and a lustral chamber. The chamber has a basin that is thought to have been used as a place of ritual cleansing, but some scholars have argued that the lustral chamber was simply a domestic bathroom.

At the larger city of Phaistos the palace was oriented in a north south direction atop a spectacular peak. At the heart of the palace complex was a central court measuring over 150 feet by 75 feet, with the court's corridors, accessed through porticoes, leading to various precincts of the palace. The central court provided a picturesque view of Mount Ida, which may have been venerated as a sacred peak. Regardless, the orientation of the complex at Phaistos was undoubtedly established to take account of the position of the revered mountain.

The palace was entered from the west court via an impressive extant 40 foot wide staircase that led to a generous platform in front of what is supposed to have been a grand portico entrance. The elevation of this portio is impossible to reconstruct, as only the footings remain. The storerooms of the palace at Phaistos are located to the south of the main gate and were quite extensive, as is common elsewhere in Minoan palace architecture. The ten rooms flanked a central corridor connecting them all. The north east wing contained the workshops of artisans while the west wing seems to have been devoted to religious observations. Among the structures with religious functions are some Pillar Crypts, lower rooms with benches and a pillar or tree in the center, objects venerated by the Minoans. Nearby are rooms with lustral basins. In the north wing of the palace are the so called Royal Apartments.

Ruins of the Palace at Phaistos. Photo: Jerzy Strzelecki

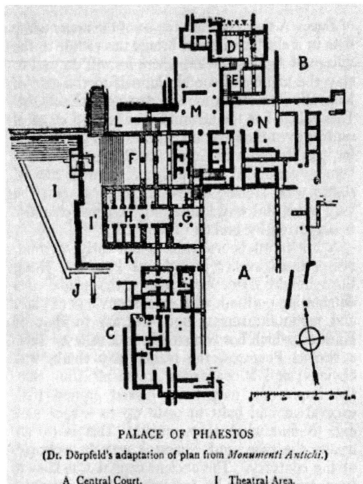

PALACE OF PHAESTOS

(Dr. Dörpfeld's adaptation of plan from *Monumenti Antichi.*)

A Central Court.
B North-east Section.
C Domestic Quarters.
D Outer Megaron.
E Inner Megaron.
F Hall of State.
G Men's Megaron.
H Magazines.

I Theatral Area.
I' West Court.
J South-west Entrance
K Main Corridor.
L Balcony.
M Peristyle Court.
N Inner Court.

At Mallia, the remains of the second palace, built about 1750 BCE and destroyed a century later, reveal a structure similar the palaces in the other cities. Again, a large court about 150 by 75 feet is at the center of the palace, but this palace had an altar in the middle of the court, which a unique feature. East of the court are six storerooms which would have held large *pithoi* or storage jars set on raised platforms along the sides of the long narrow rooms. In the center of each of the storerooms, a channel leads to a drain, which was probably used to collect spillage of olive oil and/or wine.

On the north side of the court was a large slightly elevated building with a loggia facing the court. It is likely that this building was the site of religious ceremonies. Behind it was the Treasure Room. On the west side of the central court was the main hall that served as a venue for religious services. A pillar crypt was accessed through an entrance off the main court. Because Minoan pillar crypts are relatively small and did not require a central column to support the roof beams like other larger buildings, it is assumed by some archaeologists that there was some religious function to the pillars in these rooms. The idea that the column has a religious purpose in Minoan architecture is supported by the existence of eight large, circular column bases just outside the palace at Mallia. If these structures were not religious in purpose, they may have had a function in water conservation or grain storage. On the north side of the central court was the formal entrance to the Royal Apartments. They are located beyond what has been identified as a banqueting hall.

Ruins at the Palace of Mallia

The largest and best documented Minoan palace is the one at Knossos, which was excavated and partly rebuilt by Arthur Evans. Evans discovered that what he called the New Palace at Knossos was built over an earlier structure constructed in the third millennium BCE The New

Palace, built around 1700 BCE, was an elaborate structure that contained storerooms in the west wing and one of the most impressive spaces that Evans called the Throne Room.

The "Throne Room" of the Palace of Knossos

An entrance of four openings between piers leads down to an antechamber that was flanked by low benches. From this room one entered the Throne Rome, which had a stone throne placed against one long wall. It was surrounded by stone benches and faced a lustrum or ritual bathing chamber that was reached by a short staircase. The walls were decorated with frescoes with brightly painted griffins. While Evans thought that the throne he found was the earliest royal chair in Europe, it seems this ceremonial throne was more likely used by a priestess who sat among her colleagues and re-enacted the divine manifestation of the "Lady of the Labyrinth", the chief Minoan goddess.

Figurines of the Snake Goddess

To the south of the Throne Room was a chamber called the Snake Goddess Sanctuary, where Evans found a glazed earthenware image what he termed the Snake Goddess. Further on, the Temple of the Repositories yielded a number of images of the Snake Goddess that had been buried in the ground. Also in the west wing was the Cup Bearer Sanctuary, with frescoes of bearers of conical rhytons or ritual vessels used for offering liquid to the gods. A number of long narrow storerooms are also found in the west wing, apparently used to store tall pithoi (about 5 feet high earthenware vases with incised decorative patterns) that contained oil, wine and perhaps grain. Above these storage rooms was what Evans called the Great Sanctuary, which may have served as a venue for the public display of religious ceremonies.

Evans' Reconstruction of Inner Gateway of the North Entrance of Palace at Knossos

One of the formal entrances to the Palace at Knossos was to the north. Beyond the entrance was the North Pillar Hall which may have served as a kind of anteroom or waiting room. It connected with the Bull Chamber, so named because it was decorated with a bull relief fresco.

The East Wing of the Palace contained workshops and a sanctuary of the Great Goddess on the second story that was accessed by means of a staircase from the central court. A grand staircase descended through two colonnaded landings down to the Hall of the Double Axes. Evans identified this area of the Palace as the Royal Apartments. Close by the Hall of the Double Axes is the Dolphin Sanctuary, so called because it contained a fresco showing bright blue Dolphins swimming in a sea surrounded by fish and sea urchins. Evans named this area of the palace the Queen's Apartment.

Dolphin fresco

Minoan Religion

Fresco of Dancing Women. Photo: Cavorite

If the persuasive (and now possibly predominant) argument among scholars that the great Minoan palaces were religious structures rather than centers of secular royal administration is accurate, then it is clear that religion itself was at the center of Minoan culture. The presence of storerooms, archives, treasuries and crafts workshops in the "palace" complexes, along with the types of decoration and architecture, do indeed indicate that the culture of the Minoans was organized around religion. In the absence of any evidence that Minoan society was structured around a priest king, a position of religious and secular power commonly found in other Bronze Age cultures of the Near East, it is possible that the Minoans were uniquely religiocentric.

A statue from the 7th century BCE that is believed to depict Potnia

The principal Minoan goddess was Potnia, or "The Lady", as she was designated in the inscribed tablets found in the archives of Minoan cities. She is the chief guardian of households and cities, and the primary symbol of Potnia was the double-axe. This kind of axe was called *labrys* in Greek. It is likely that the word, like its cognate labyrinth, made its way into Greek from the language of the Minoans. The double headed axe appears frequently in Minoan temple decoration, in frescoes, and in incised reliefs, and large numbers of bronze symbolic axes have been unearthed.

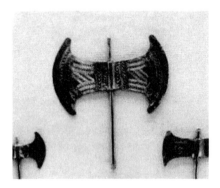

Bronze Double-Axe Ritual Object at the Heraklion Archaeological Museum

Photo: Wolfgang Sauber

Potnia also may have been symbolized by the pillar and the snake, both of which seemed to carry special reverence among the Minoans. At Knossos there is an inscription that records an offering to "Potnia of the Labyrinth", suggesting that a temple to her existed in the "palace" complex.

How Potnia was related to other gods and goddesses in the Minoan pantheon is difficult to determine. Was she the embodiment of all the lesser gods, or did they exist on an equal plane with her? There was a separate deity, or, perhaps just a separate figurative manifestation of Potnia herself, that has been identified as a goddess of fertility and procreation. This deity was represented by a dove. Another goddess or another side of Potnia was the patron of seasonal renewal in nature. Renewal also was assisted by a young male spirit called Velchanos.

Other distinct goddesses who may have evolved over the millennia from various aspects or manifestations of Potnia was the Mistress of Wild Animals, known as Britomartis among the Minoans. Britomartis was also known as the Sweet Virgin, who, it is surmised, evolved into the classical Greek goddess Artemis, the huntress.

Britomartis had a male counterpart called Master of Animals, whose symbols were a shield and spear. It is likely that the cow hide shields depicted in a fresco at Knossos are not military symbols but represent the Master of Animals.

The Minoans not only invoked their gods and goddesses in temples included in the palace complexes of cities, but they also made offerings to them in hilltop and cave shrines, several of which have been excavated in Crete. Briomartis, her male companion, and the goddess of childbirth Eleuthia seem to have been particularly venerated in these remote shrines.

The Minoan universal spirit, Potnia, manifested herself also as a tree goddess. In this guise she was venerated at pillar and tree shrines found in all the major Minoan cities. Further she appears as a Snake Goddess, a deity of the underworld, in artworks unearthed at Knossos where she brandishes snakes in her out-held hands.

From frescoes, seals and other artworks it is clear that religious ceremonies involved dance, and it is assumed that priestesses in these dances first impersonated a goddess and then came to assume a role in which they were considered actual incarnations of the divinities. One of the many religious ceremonies of the Minoans that has captivated archaeologists, scholars and the general public is bull leaping. This acrobatic and possibly dangerous way of honoring the divine has been the subject of considerable speculation.

   In the central court of Minoan cities, young athletes (perhaps female as well as male), performed some kind of spectacular dance with a bull. Several interpretations of the bull-leaping ceremony have been put forward based on the depiction of the ceremony in Minoan art, particularly on several seals, some metalwork, and a fresco at Knossos. Evans believed that the leapers grasped the bull's horns and vaulted and summersaulted over the bulls back to land upright either on the back of the bull or on the ground by its tail. Some have argued that this feat of athleticism would've been nearly impossible, and that what the Minoans did was more like modern Spanish bull fighting. Whatever the truth of the matter is, bull-leaping offers a fascinating glimpse of Minoan worship, and it suggests that the Minoans combined sport, dance, and athleticism as part of their religious ceremonies. That combination is a forerunner to the religious aspect of classical Greek athletic competitions at Olympia, the Olympics. The common use of stylized bull horns in the decoration of Knossos, in particular on the cresting of buildings, were constant reminders of the importance of the bull within the religious precinct of the city.

Minoan Art

Griffin Fresco in the Throne Room at the Palace of Knossos

Perhaps the most lasting legacy left by the Minoans on the European civilizations that followed them was their art. In Minoan society, the arts and crafts were held in particularly high regard, and it was so apparent during early excavations that the chronology of Minoan civilization is demarcated by the changes in their pottery. Moreover, it seems Minoan art was one of their most valuable trading resources, judging from the findings of Minoan artwork in the ruins of Bronze Age or Helladic Era cities in mainland Greece (part of the Mycenaean Civilization) and the Cyclades and in the Middle East (particularly in Egypt).

Considering the Minoans' capacity to create intricate, beautifully designed art in a variety of ways, all of which demonstrated a highly developed aesthetic and mastery of many often complicated techniques, it is not surprising that they considered art an important, perhaps the most important, avenue in religious expression. In the palaces or temple complexes excavated to date, there are rooms that clearly served as workshops for craftsmen. Remains of looms, bits of carved ivory and pottery shards indicate the that different workshops were dedicated to different crafts of art.

The centrality of art to Minoan culture is also readily obvious in the fact that the buildings at Knossos were brightly colored; Evans even painted his reconstructed columns of the Palace at Knossos red. In the interior spaces, columns shaped like upturned trees that got narrower from the top to bottom were painted and topped by colorful capitals. Ancient Greek columns and the columns that followed got narrower from bottom to top, which is a more practical design in an engineering sense, because columns with a thicker base can support more weight. The fact that the Minoans' columns had it the other way around suggests their purpose was not simply for practical engineering. The columns supported brightly painted ceiling beams that divided the intricately patterned wooden ceiling into squares and rectangles, a kind of colorful decoration that was repeated both inside the buildings and outside.

The walls of some of the rooms were decorated with large frescoes, with such themes as stylized griffins in the so -called Throne Room, and elsewhere with pictures of ritual dancers, bull leapers and dolphins swimming in the sea. The skill of the Minoan painters is not only clearly evident in their careful composition of the scenes and their pleasing use of line and color but also in the technique of their execution - true fresco. The painters worked on wet plaster applied to the stone walls of the rooms. This required quick painting, before the plaster dried, and thus precise planning of each image must have been undertaken before work could begin.

The same sense of form and design and technical expertise is evident in Minoan pottery painting. Patterns, birds, fish and other animals were depicted on Minoan pots in such a way as to utilize the form of the pottery to enhance the impact of the decoration. Some have considered the apogee of Minoan pottery painting to be their Marine Style works that are typified by a wonderfully animated octopus that stretches its many arms over a vessel. One of the many treasures of Minoan painting is the Hagia Triada sarcophagus of about 1400 BCE excavated at a villa not far from Phaistos. It shows a procession of people carrying offerings to an altar. The figures are dressed in ceremonial garb are quite lifelike. They are rhythmically dispersed in a frieze that is enclosed in a brightly painted patterned frame.

Pottery dated between 2100-1700 BCE

In addition to painting, the Minoans excelled in ivory and stone carving. An ivory figure of a bull leaper, found at Knossos and dated around 1600 BCE, is a remarkable example of the fragile but elegant work the Minoans were capable of. The survival of Minoan sculpture in ivory is extremely rare, but a few examples still exist, including one of a group of two goddesses and a divine child dating from the 14th century BCE found in mainland Greece at Mycenae. This work showed that the carvers of Crete were capable of creating moving work that captured not only intricate interaction of human figures but even human emotion. Incorporating facial expressions and emotion in art was fully popularized by the Ancient Greeks nearly a millennium later.

Bee pendant from Mallia

Minoan craftsmen also displayed unusual talent when working with metals. A well known example of their metalwork is an exquisite bee pendant found at Mallia, which dates back to about 1500 BCE In this piece, two bees are arranged facing each other around a honey comb. Their enlarged outstretched wings are decorated with pendants, above their heads is a tiny wire-enclosed ball, and another pendant hangs from where their curved abdomens meet. The artist who made this pendant not only understood the principles of great design; he also had a very good understanding of the form of bees through careful observation of them in nature.

The best known Minoan metalworks are the two Vapheio Cups found in a tomb near Sparta on the Greek mainland. These items were so highly prized by their owner, who acquired them in trade or possibly bought them from a traveling Cretan craftsman, that he had them interred with him so he could enjoy them in the afterlife. The gold cups are decorated with narrative reliefs. On one of the cups, a bull is shown trapped in a net on one side, and on the other side the bull is shown trampling his captors and escaping their clutches. The second cup shows a bull being caught through the use of a decoy cow. The sophisticated reliefs of the Vapheio Cups show that Minoan artists were adept at creating the illusion of space and skilled in recreating the animal's anatomy.

Vapheio Cup

While the examples of artwork in ivory and metal are relatively rare, thankfully the same cannot be said of Minoan seals, of which many existed. The Minoans used seals to ensure security for items of trade. Containers such as the pithoi found in the storerooms in the palaces would be capped and sealed to indicate ownership and to prevent tampering. However, what truly interests observers today is the artwork. Minoan seals can be seen in museums around the world, and they have received considerable attention by scholars. Arthur Evans in particular was drawn to the minute detail of Minoan seal carving.

Seals have been categorized based on their shape, including lentoid, oval, square, and other shapes. The seals were carved from different materials depending on their age, including bone, ivory, steatite, carnelian and agate for earlier seals. In the later Minoan period from 1700 BCE and on, seals were carved from jasper, chalcedony, lapis, hematite, amethyst and obsidian, and the shapes included cylinder, cone, prism or signet ring.

Minoan seals have an unbelievable array of designs that provide a kind of encyclopaedic picture of Minoan society. Motifs include animals, human figures, proto-heraldic designs, symbols and lettering, ships, buildings, goddesses and religious ceremonies. The subjects of Minoan seals are more often than not so carefully rendered that they provide a view of civilization that is unequalled in the ancient world. From these seals comes an excellent picture of what a Minoan ship looked like, what a Minoan hunt was like, how the Minoans worshipped, what the Minoans wore and other aspects of Minoan life.

Minoan Seal depicting Bull-Leaping

Life in a Minoan City

Based on excavations at Knossos, Zakros, Mallia, Phaistos and Gournia, scholars can confidently assert that Minoan cities were densely packed with houses that lined narrow streets. There were also highly developed water and wastewater systems that ran in a network beneath the surface of the streets.

The large palace or temple complexes were constructed using a variety of building materials. In the interior on the ground floor, the typical building used finely cut gypsum covered with stucco (and in some rooms frescoes). The gypsum blocks were set within a framework of wood beams, which was probably a technique that reduced the damage caused by earthquakes. The floors were of finely polished gypsum and the ceilings were made of wood planks running between large wood beams. The second story was usually constructed with mud brick that was also set in a wood beam framework.

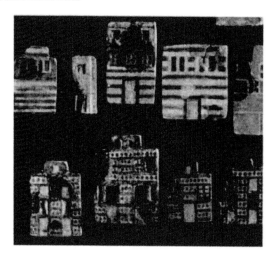

Faience Tablets showing House Facades at Knossos, from the Palace of Knossos

Domestic housing was two or three stories in height, constructed in a similar manner with limestone blocks on the ground floor and mud brick above. A series of faience or glazed earthenware plaques found at Knossos indicates the facades of the urban houses were patterned, which certainly would have given a decorative enhancement to the streetscape.

The organization of Minoan society, and what if any social hierarchies there were, remains unclear. This is largely due to the fact that the first writing system of the Minoans continues to baffle scholars. The language, which has been called Linear A, is found on many of the inscribed tablets unearthed throughout the Minoan world. The second language used by the Minoans, Linear B, was deciphered by Michael Ventris, who discovered in 1952 that the language was an early version of Greek. The texts of the Linear B tablets reveal many details of Minoan life, but without being able to decipher Linear A, some aspects of Minoan life remain in the dark. That said, while the texts of Linear A still baffle scholars, they have given us a clear picture of the Minoan numerical system. It was a simple decimal system without the use of zero, paralleling that used by the ancient Egyptians.

What we know of the appearance of the Minoans is largely derived from art that depicts their religious ceremonies. From the frescoes and from sculpture and seals, at least in the context of these religious ceremonies, Minoan females had long hair that was curled and held in place behind the ears by jewelry. Make-up was used to enhance the eyes. In religious ceremonies, the men and women wore robes of blue, orange or white that were decorated with bands of colour and tied at the waist by a belt or cord. In some examples of Minoan art, figures that have been identified as priestesses wore a more elaborate double garment. The bodice was cut low, revealing the breasts, and the skirt had a vertical slit that revealed a braid-decorated undergarment. The priestesses wearing this kind of double skirt are shown with elaborate headdresses and rich jewelry. Males shown in the context of religious ceremonies sometimes wear a feather headdress and are naked except for a belted loincloth and a codpiece which was worn over it. The loincloth might be striped or patterned.

The life of Minoans involved in agricultural production is known partially through inscribed Linear B tablets. In one set of tablets found at Knossos, the names of ox-drivers and the names of the oxen they used to plough the fields were listed. The crops grown by the Minoans included wheat, spelt and barley, all of which were recorded in the tablets under the generic term "grain". The farmers used axes, adzes and sickles made of bronze and used simple wagons for the transport of harvested crops. Threshing was done on a stone platform and the grain was winnowed by being tossed into the air with the aid of winnowing forks.

Other crops grown by the Minoan farmers included chick peas, sesame, flax, figs, quince, dates, grapes and olives. Olive oil was used for cooking, washing and lighting. Livestock included goats, sheep, cattle and pigs, and Minoan food was sweetened with honey, which itself was a major crop and a frequent offering at the palace temple. Presumably for use in food preparation and in religious ceremonies, the Minoans harvested the abundant varieties of herbs and spices that grew on the hillsides and in the valleys of Crete.

The one natural resource that the Minoans harvested in quantity was timber. It was used liberally in the construction of their homes and temples and was critical in the building of boats along several coastal towns. It has been argued by some historians that the Minoans were so zealous in their use of timber that the consequent land erosion put the very existence of their civilization in peril.

The Minoan Empire

Minoan economy expanded over the years because they controlled a vast trade network, the full extent of which is not precisely known. However, it is clear from finds in Egyptian tombs and sites elsewhere in the Middle East that the Minoans' sea-empire was incredibly widespread, perhaps stretching from modern Spain to Syria and Egypt. Findings in Egyptian tombs include representations of Minoan vessels in art, particularly on seals, and one appears in an Egyptian tomb painting. The Minoan ships varied in size, from quite modest coastal vessels to larger ships with a mast in the middle supporting a square sail. As many as 15 oars on each side were used to propel the ship on windless days. Some of the art depicts Minoan ships that had high prows and sterns and were steered by a single oar managed from a deck at the stern. The ships are shown with cabins amidship or at the stern. Excavations at Minoan seaports on Crete, at places like

Kydonia, Rethymnon, and Amnisos, have also shed some light on Minoan maritime commerce and shipbuilding.

The exact nature and extent of the Minoan empire is not clearly understood at present. There seem to have been colonial cities established around the eastern Mediterranean and on the islands of the Aegean, including Kythera, Naxos, Rhodes, Iasos and Miletus. The relationship between these towns and cities with the cities on Crete is not entirely clear. They may have been vassal city states, or they may have been equal trade partners. The most significant find of a Minoan colony is at Akrotiri on the island of Thera. There were probably Minoan colonies on mainland Greece as well.

The extent of Minoan trading is evidenced by decorative art that has been found in archaeological sites around the Mediterranean. In addition to exporting fine crafts, the Minoans sent timber and woolen cloth to Egypt in exchange for linen and possibly papyrus. It is likely that the Minoans exported surplus olive oil and grain in trade for exotic materials used in the production of luxury goods, such as copper from Sardinia and Etruscan tin from Italy. Tin may even have been imported from as far away as Britain, and there is evidence that some amber found at Knossos may have come from southwest England.

The Minoans also traded their excess wine and olive oil with the Myceneans on mainland Greece and imported a vast array of goods including minerals such as black obsidian from Anatolia, lapis lazuli from Syria (originally brought from Afganistan), and amethyst and carnelian from Egypt. Egyptian beads and scarabs have been found in some Cretan sites as well.

The End of Minoan Culture

The power of the Minoan civilization and its commercial dominance in the Mediterannean came to an abrupt halt around 1400-1500 BCE Archeologists have found evidence that many of the Cretan cities suffered severe damage and were ravaged by fire at the same time Minoan trade diminished. Although some of the cities were reoccupied and partially rebuilt, the Minoan civilization never fully recovered. There is evidence that the Myceneans from the mainland began to occupy the cities of Crete and became the dominant traders in the Eastern Mediterranean.

What caused this sudden collapse of the vibrant civilization of the Minoans? Throughout the late 19th century and much of the 20th century, some scholars believed the Minoans were unable to maintain their dominance over the bellicose Myceneans, while others speculated the growth of the Minoan population could not be supported by the agricultural production of Crete.

However, recent archaeological finds have led to a consensus among scholars that the Minoan civilization was destroyed by a natural cataclysm. The Greek philosopher Plato, in two of his dialogues, relates a legend concerning the complete destruction of a fabulous city called Atlantis. It was, he said, "swallowed up by the sea and vanished". This tale has intrigued generations of treasure hunters and enthusiasts of mysticism who have taken the legend at face value. It seems increasingly clear, however, that the story of the destruction of Atlantis as told by Plato is one based on fact with the exaggeration attendant on oral tradition.

Excavations at Akrotiri on the island of Thera (Santorini) to the north of Crete have revealed a city buried under a deep layer of volcanic ash. While only a fraction of the large city has been unearthed to date, the enormous number of artifacts and the incredible frescoes that have been revealed indicate that this city was a Minoan settlement of great magnificence. The volcanic ash that rained down on this city was produced by the vast eruption of a volcano that destroyed most of the island of Thera. The explosion has been generally dated to the 17th or 16th century BCE, but based on more recent study the eruption occurred between 1627 and 1600 BCE Calculations of the size of the eruption from measurements of the dispersal of its ash in the eastern Mediterranean and the study of tree rings that show a period of diminished growth on account of atmospheric ash indicate that the explosion at Thera was an unbelievably powerful event. It caused a great tidal wave, estimated to have been over 35 feet high when it crashed into the north coast of Crete, and it shook the region with powerful earthquakes. The tidal wave would have destroyed the Minoan port towns of Crete, including Mallia, while earthquakes would have severely damaged Knossos and the other palace cities of Crete. It is quite likely that the damage was so extensive that the cities would have become uninhabitable, and the temporary climate change caused by the volcano may have resulted in severe crop reduction.

With the catastrophic damage to their cities, their agriculture and their maritime trade, the Minoans that survived and eventually reoccupied their cities could not restore them to their former glory. The weakened Minoan culture became easy prey to formerly secondary powers, with anthropologists believing that tribes from mainland Greece and Phoenician seafarers invaded Crete and filled the vacuum in Mediterranean maritime trade.

Whatever the case, despite the quick collapse of the Minoan civilization, it's clear that they continued to hold a special place among their neighbors, with their culture continuing to be passed down in story and culture among the Ancient Greeks. And it's safe to assume that the "first link in the European chain" will continue to fascinate the world well into the future.

The Background of the Mycenaeans

The ethnic-linguistic background of the Mycenaeans was Indo-European, like their Hittite contemporaries and most of the people who would later populate Europe, and they were war-like invaders similar to various Indo-European tribes. (Anthony 2007, 12) The Indo-European ancestors of the Mycenaeans entered Greece around 2200 BCE and pillaged the countryside while they worked their way south, as is evidenced by burn levels at known settlements from the period (Samuel 1966, 37).

Eventually these Indo-European invaders settled down, and by around 1500 BCE they began to build the first known cities in Europe. The most important Mycenaean cities – known by their later classical Greek names – were Mycenae, Pylos, and Tiryns. Mycenae was known in classical times for being the home of many of the heroes of the legendary Trojan War, and as the 2nd century CE Greek geographer Pausanias noted, it was the site of ruins even in his time. The geographer wrote, "In the ruins of Mycenae is a fountain called Persea; there are also underground chambers of Atreus and his children, in which were stored their treasures. There is the grave of Atreus, along with the graves of such as returned with Agamemnon from Troy, and were murdered by Aegisthus after he had given them a banquet." (Pausanias, II, XVI, 6). The modern discovery and importance of this tomb will be discussed later, but the relevance of Mycenae is clear in that the ruins were still a marvel to the classical Greeks hundreds of years later.

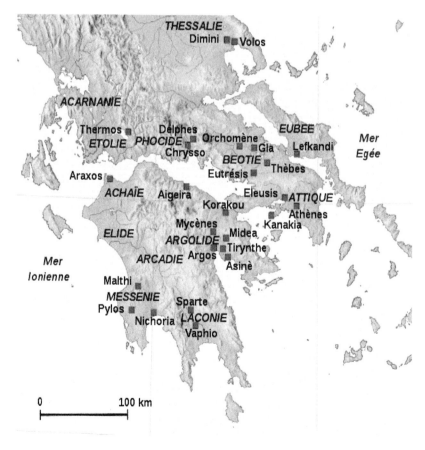

A map of Greece during the Mycenaean era

The cultural importance of Mycenae in the Bronze Age may actually have been equaled by Pylos. Pylos has been described by modern scholars as the "corporate headquarters of the Late Bronze Age Peloponnese" because it was the center of much economic activity and the site where many of the Mycenaean Linear B tablets have been discovered, most of which concern business transactions (Samuel 1966, 2). Both Pausanias and the Greek-Roman geographer Strabo gave descriptions of Pylos in their writings; part of Pausanias' description reads, "Of Pylus in the land of Elis the ruins are to be seen on the mountain road from Olympia to Elis, the distance between Elis and Pylus being eighty stades. This Pylus was founded, as I have already said, by a Megarian called Pylon, the son of Cleson. Destroyed by Heracles and refounded by the Eleans, the city was doomed in time to be without inhabitants. Beside it the river Ladon flows into the Peneius. The Eleans declare that there is a reference to this Pylus in the passage of Homer." (Pausanias, VI, XXII, 4-5).

Pylos was also mentioned by Strabo, who wrote that its location was near Elis, which was finally confirmed by archeological excavations of the site in 1907 (Preziosi and Hitchcock 1999, 155). Modern excavations of Pylos have revealed that the city was centered around a large palace that was built during the archeological period known as the Late Halladic IIA (ca. 1300 BCE) and was destroyed between 1230-1200 BCE, which would coincide with the general migrations and destructions associated with the Sea Peoples at the end of the Bronze Age. The architecture of Pylos closely resembles early Minoan architecture on Crete, which again points to the idea of the Mycenaeans carrying the torch of Aegean civilization that was initially lit by the Minoans. (Preziosi and Hitchcock 1999, 156). Interestingly, the Mycenaean palace of Pylos is the only one that can be positively identified by modern scholars as such through Linear B tablets (Preziosi and Hitchcock 1999, 160).

Alun Salt's picture of a Mycenaean tomb in Pylos

Pylos' greatness approached and probably even surpassed that of Mycenae, but the classical Greek authors also wrote of another Mycenaean city: Tiryns. Tiryns may not have had the commercial importance of Pylos or the name recognition of Mycenae, but the walls that its people built impressed Greek and Roman travelers centuries later. According to Strabo, the mythical Proetus used the city as a home: "Now it seems that Tiryns was used as a base of operations by Proetus, and was walled by him through the aid of the Cyclopes, who were seven in number, and were called 'Bellyhands' because they got their food from their handicraft, and they came by invitation from Lycia. And perhaps the caverns near Nauplia and the works therein are named after them. The acropolis, Licymna, is named after Licymnius, and it is about twelve stadia distant from Nauplia; but it is deserted, and so is the neighbouring Midea, which is different from the Boetian Midea." (Strabo, VIII, 6, 11).

Strabo's description of Tiryns being built by Cyclopes may seem strange, fanciful, and maybe even a bit superstitious to modern readers, but one must remember that the classical Greeks and Romans knew nothing of modern archeological techniques, and their historical methods were sometimes unsophisticated to say the least. When viewed from that perspective, it is more understandable that they attributed great walls of an unknown origin to a mythological race of creatures. To the Greeks and Romans, the only people before them who attained a reasonable level of advancement were the Egyptians and Mesopotamians, so any great monuments built before the classical Greeks, especially in Greece, were often attributed to the divine.

Nick Stenning's picture of part of Tiryns' walls

Mycenaean Religion

The divine clearly played an important role in the lives of the Mycenaeans, just as it did with later classical Greeks, but when scholars attempt to reconstruct different facets of Mycenaean religion, many of the same impediments are encountered that plague accurate reconstructions of Mycenaean chronology. Presently, no great temples or religious edifices are known to have been built by the Mycenaeans, which has led some modern scholars to suggest that Mycenaean society was "not theologically orientated." (Samuel 1964, 94). That said, the fact that no temples have been discovered yet does not mean that archeologists will not locate one or more in the future, and the absence of temples does not necessarily mean the Mycenaeans were not religious or theologically driven people. Moreover, while some of the Mycenaeans' contemporaries (such as the Egyptians and Mesopotamians) built great temples to their gods, and many religious sanctuaries were built on Crete by the Minoans, that does not mean that the Mycenaeans eschewed all religious practices and/or observations by comparison. With the exception of the Minoans, Mycenaean culture was fundamentally different than the other cultures of the Bronze Age Mediterranean, so to simply say that theirs was not a theocracy is a simplistic conclusion at best.

When historians examine the primary sources in their totality, a clearer image of Mycenaean religion can be reached, and it is one of a people who honored their gods in many unique ways. The Linear B tablets from Pylos provide modern scholars with a glimpse into the names of some of the Mycenaean deities, as well as the context in which they were worshipped. Indeed, the deities are mentioned in the tablets exclusively as recipients of offerings, which indicates that the Mycenaeans practiced an active, ritual based religion much like their contemporaries in the Mediterranean (Chadwick 1973, 125).

Perhaps most notably, the head of the Greek pantheon, Zeus, is mentioned in tablets from Pylos, while Poseidon, the Greek god of the seas, is mentioned in tablets from both Pylos and the Cretan city of Knossos (Chadwick 1973, 125-6). The worship of Zeus and Poseidon – both of whom played important roles in later classical Greek myth and religion – is interesting but not at all extraordinary when one considers that the Mycenaeans were ethnic Greeks and that many of their gods came from an Indo-European source. Zeus shared similar attributes with the Indic god Indra and the Norse god Thor for example, and the name "Zeus" itself is probably a cognate of the Hittite god "Sius" (Anthony 2007, 262). The importance of Poseidon to the Mycenaeans should not be overlooked either, and it makes a lot of sense since sea trade and warfare were important aspects of Mycenaean culture.

Although the exact nature of the king's role in Mycenaean religious rituals is not known, the tablets from Pylos suggest that there was a sizable priesthood that owned land and was undoubtedly powerful in its own right (Chadwick 1973, 128).

It's unclear whether the Mycenaeans ever constructed temples, but they built a number of sizable tombs that modern scholars believe may have provided a focal point for some of their religious ceremonies. Besides the palaces, the largest Mycenaean structures that have survived until the present in some degree are the large beehive tombs, which are known as tholos tombs. The tholos tombs were first built during the Late Bronze Age II period in western and central Greece (Preziosi and Hitchcock 199, 175). The tholos style then spread to Mycenae itself, where it reached its apex with the so-called "Treasury of Arteus."

Entrance to the Treasury of Arteus

Carlos Prieto's picture of the interior of the Treasury of Arteus

Since ancient writers such as Pausanias were unaware of the scope and nuances of Mycenaean culture, they often assigned pre-classical monuments, such as the tholos tomb at Mycenae, to the semi-legendary characters in the Homeric epics. In fact, by the time Pausanias wrote about the great tholos tomb at Mycenae, local legend and tradition had assessed that the tomb was used as a treasury during the era of the Trojan War. Since the tholos tombs were the most prominent structures built during the height of Mycenaean power (ca. 1400-1200 BC), they no doubt served partly as symbols of wealth and power (Preziosi and Hitchcock 1999, 175).

The size and workmanship of the tombs shows that the Mycenaeans had a concern that the dead be well housed and also seems to suggest that there was some type of cult of the dead (Samuel 1966, 95). Large, monumental tombs are indicative of a people who had a well-articulated concept of the afterlife, like the ancient Egyptians, but unfortunately, since no Mycenaean documents concerning the afterlife are known to exist, modern scholars cannot say for certain how complex their theology was.

The impressive tholos tombs give modern scholars some indication of how important burial rituals, and possibly the afterlife, were in Mycenaean religion, but another archeological discovery may help fill in more gaps. The "Hagia Triada Sarcophagus," named for the city near where it was discovered on the island of Crete, is an elegantly decorated sarcophagus that may reveal some aspects of Minoan and Mycenaean burial practices and their beliefs in the afterlife. Although the sarcophagus was discovered on the island of Crete and the art is done in a Minoan style, it is dated to the period when the Mycenaeans dominated the island (Preziosi and Hitchcock 199, 178).

The Hagia Triada Sarcophagus

In the center, three men are depicted carrying what appears to be models of sacrificed animals and possibly a model of a boat towards what is likely the deceased individual (Preziosi and Hitchcock 1999, 179). The boat model is interesting because it suggests a similarity with the Egyptians, who buried their kings with boat models of different sizes (the most well-known is the life-sized boat buried next to Khufu's pyramid). The scenes on the sarcophagus clearly depict a celebration, which was made perpetual through its artistic representation, of funerary rituals and beliefs (Preziosi and Hitchcock 1999, 180). It is not much of a leap to suggest that people who created such fine works of art in a mortuary context had a belief in the afterlife.

One final aspect of Mycenaean religion that needs to be considered was also conducted in a funerary context: funeral games. The classical Greeks and Romans are well known for their gamesmanship and athletic competitions, from the Olympic Games of the Greeks to the chariot races and gladiatorial games of the Romans. Some of these events continue to both awe and outrage modern sensibilities, but many of the games of the Greeks and Romans can ultimately be traced back to the Mycenaeans, who performed these games not for large audiences but for dead kings and warriors. The size of the tholos tombs suggest that elaborate funerary rituals accompanied the internment of the deceased, and most modern scholars believe that athletic events were at least occasionally part of those rituals (Kyle 2007, 50).

Unfortunately, there are no extant Linear B inscriptions that detail Mycenaean funeral games, but Homer's *Iliad* suggests that there was a Bronze Age tradition of funerary games in Greece (Kyle 2007, 55). Since Homer lived hundreds of years after the collapse of the Mycenaean culture, his epics should not be considered as a perfect source of Mycenaean era history; but his vivid descriptions of the funeral games to honor the slain Achaean/Mycenaean/Greek warrior Patroclus reveals that the poet's contemporary society treated aristocratic funeral games as sports, even as the Greeks were transitioning to non-funerary games (Kyle 2007, 56-57).

The funerary games are detailed in book 23 of the *Iliad*, which provides modern readers with a sense of not only how the Mycenaeans honored their dead nobles and warriors but also how those games influenced classical Greek and Roman ideas of sport. This part of the epic is primarily concerned with the plethora of funeral games that the hero Achilles coordinates for his dead comrade Patroclus. After Patroclus was put to rest on a funeral pyre, Achilles held the other Mycenaeans where they were, and Homer wrote, "But Achilles held the armies on the spot. He had them sit in a great and growing circle – now for funeral games – and brought from his ships the trophies for the contests: cauldrons and tripods, stallions, mules and cattle with massive heads, women sashed and lovely, and gleaming gay iron." (Homer, The *Iliad*, 23, 300)

In total, there were eight events: a chariot race, boxing, wrestling, a foot race, armed combat, an iron toss, archery, and a javelin toss. The most "Mycenaean" of all the events was probably the chariot race, which also comprised the most verses in the book (Homer, The *Iliad*, 23, 300-720). Although little is known of how the Mycenaeans used chariots in battle, Linear B documents indicate the value they placed on the vehicles. Also, one only has to look at the Mycenaeans' contemporaries, most notably the Hittites and Egyptians, to see how important chariots were in Bronze Age warfare (Drews 1993, 104-34). The chariot was not only a prized battle vehicle in the Bronze Age but also a symbol of power and prestige for those who possessed them, as numerous diplomatic documents from the period can attest. In fact, by the time of Homer in the 9th century BCE, chariots had largely become obsolete, which further demonstrates that the extensive coverage given to the chariot race in the *Iliad* was probably an accurate custom of their funeral games.

Mycenaean Sporting Events

The other events depicted in Book 23 of the *Iliad* may seem like typical classical Greek sporting events, but closer examination reveals that they too sprang from a Mycenaean source. Boxing and wrestling were both common classical Greek sporting events that made an appearance in Book 23, but with some slight alterations that may show their Mycenaean origin. In both events, which comprise almost 100 verses combined, the men wore loincloths (zoma) and the boxers wrapped their hands with ox-hide thongs (himantes), which is distinct from the nude events the Greeks competed in during classical times (Kyle 2007, 61).

The wrestling match between the two heroes Ajax and Odysseus is described by Homer: "Both champions, belted tight, stepped into the ring and grappling each other hard with big burly arms, locked like rafters a master builder bolts together, slanting into a pitched roof to fight the ripping winds." (Homer, The *Iliad*, 23, 780-790).

As the two heroes struggled to pin each other, Achilles, ever the mindful commander and always a warrior first, stopped the contest before it turned to bloodshed. "No more struggling – don't kill yourselves in sport! Victory goes to both. Share the prizes. Off you go, so the rest of the men can have a crack at contests." (Homer, The Iliad, 23, 820).

Although both heroes were awarded prizes for the wrestling event, they apparently still needed to whet their competitive spirit some more. Ajax and Odysseus would have a rematch during the foot race, perhaps the most quintessential of all Greek sporting events, and in the course of the race, Homer displays a bit of a sense of humor and mythology at the same time. "Athena tripped him up – right where the dung lay slick from bellowing cattle the swift runner Achilles slew in Patroclus' honor. Dung stuffed his mouth, his nostrils dripped much as shining long-enduring Odysseus flashed past him to come in first by far and carry off the cup while Ajax took the ox." (Homer, The Iliad, 860-5).

The other events are all essentially Greek in character and can be seen as originating during the Mycenaean period, with the exception of the iron toss and the armed battle. The iron toss was a clearly anachronistic event, as the Mycenaeans would have had little to no experience with the metal during the Bronze Age, but if the Trojan War took place during the late Bronze Age (which will be discussed below), it would have been known and fetched a premium as a prize as in the *Iliad*.

The armed event consisted of two heroes fighting each other with weapons and armor. Homer described the event as such: "But now Diomedes thrusting over the giant's massive shield, again and again, threatened to graze his throat – the spear point glinting sharp – and such terror for Ajax struck his Argive friends they cried for them to stop, to divide the prizes, 'Share and share alike!' But the hero Achilles took the great long sword and gave it to Diomedes, slung in its sheath on a supple, well-cut sword-strap." (Homer, The Iliad, 23, 910-17).

The event reads like a Roman gladiator match, which may be one of the sources of the quintessential Roman game, but the source of this and other Mycenaean sporting events may have come from the east. The sporting events described in the *Iliad* were all done in the context of funeral ceremonies and therefore religious in nature to a certain extent, but the Mycenaeans like all people before and after them performed sports and athletic events for a number of reasons, and many of the events were influenced by non-Mycenaean peoples. Historian Donald Kyle credits both the Hittites and Minoans for influencing the Mycenaeans, especially after they took over the island of Crete. (Kyle 2007, 39).

One particular similarity between Hittite and Mycenaean sports is the armed combat contest such as those described in Book 23 of the *Iliad*. As noted above, this type of event was mimicked centuries later by the Romans, but a similar event was also practiced during the Bronze Age by the Hittites, who staged mock battles by men divided into two teams: "The Men of Hatti" and "The Men of Masa" (western Anatolia) (Kyle 2007, 46). The Men of Hatti, who always won, used bronze weapons against the reed wielding Men of Masa (Kyle 2007, 47). It is difficult not to see a linear progression from that event to the armed funeral game battles described by Homer, especially when one considers the other connections between the Hittites and Mycenaeans.

The Minoan influence on Mycenaean sport may have been most prominent in boxing events. A Minoan rhyton, known as the "Boxer Rhyton," depicts two men involved in what seems to be organized fisticuffs, and although the piece lacks graphic depictions of blood (as the later Greeks and Romans were prone to show), it may represent the origin of the sport and its first depiction in Europe (Kyle 2007, 40). The importance of sport to the Mycenaeans is therefore gleaned from a number of disparate sources, which demonstrate that although the Mycenaeans may have culled at least some the events from other peoples, their contribution to sports and athletics no doubt influenced the classical Greeks and Romans.

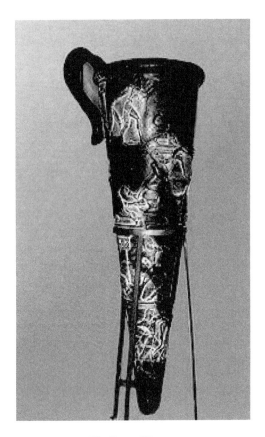

The Boxer Rhyton

Mycenaean Language and Linear B Script

Most modern historians argue that a necessary prerequisite for any society to be termed a "civilization" is the invention or adaptation of writing. Writing allows people to record their history and myths, conduct diplomacy, and to keep business and government records.

All of the great societies of the pre-modern world either created their own form of writing from scratch or adapted a script or form of writing from another people, and the Mycenaeans were no exception. The Mycenaeans employed a form of writing that is known today as Linear B script, and although inscriptions in Linear B were not as widespread and varied as those of the Mycenaeans' contemporaries in Egypt and Anatolia, it was a developed form of writing and enough texts exist that modern scholars can determine their language was essentially the same language spoken by the classical Greeks.

The route that modern scholars took to decipher Linear B script was a bit circuitous, and, as the name implies, it was preceded by another similar form of writing. The discovery of Linear B script happened by accident in 1886 when Arthur Evans, who was the preeminent archeologist of Minoan culture and keeper of the Ashmolean Museum in Oxford, was shown a seal-stone from Crete inscribed with a form of writing that was previously unknown to him (Chadwick 1973, 8). At the time, scholars knew that the Minoans on Crete used a form of writing, but they were (and still are) unable to decipher the hieroglyphic characters. Scholars eventually termed the Minoan script Linear A script, while the type of writing on the seal-stone Evans examined was determined to be a closely related but ultimately different script that was eventually labeled "Linear B." Linear A was used from about 1600-1450 BCE on Crete, while Linear B surpassed the earlier form of writing after 1450 on Crete and from approximately 1405-1200 BC on mainland Greece (Chadwick 1973, 28).

Arthur Evans

Although Linear A and B scripts were similar, as the latter was based on the former, the languages the two scripts represented were totally different, which eventually led to success in deciphering Linear B, even though attempts to decipher the Linear A script have met numerous roadblocks. This is because philologists have no idea what language family Minoan was derived from; attempts to place the Minoan language into the Indo-European, Semitic, and Afro-Asiatic language groups have all been futile, so the script still remains unreadable (Preziosi and Hitchcock 1999, 4).

It is important to point out that spoken languages and script are not mutually inclusive. For instance, English is an Indo-European language and is written in the Latin alphabet, which is also an Indo-European language, but English can just as easily be written in the Arabic script. Farsi, which is an Indo-European language, is primarily written in the Arabic script, demonstrating the type of writing people employ cannot necessarily show historians and philologists what group the language belongs in.

Meanwhile, the effort to decipher the Linear B script was a long process and involved the work and cooperation of scores of scholars, but fortunately, in 1952, Englishman Michael Ventris cracked the enigmatic code (Preziosi and Hitchcock 1999, 158-9). Ventris' efforts proved that although the form of writing the Mycenaeans used was adapted from that of the Minoans, the language itself was an early form of Greek (Chadwick 1973, 68). After Ventris' decipherment of the Linear B script historians knew unequivocally that the Mycenaeans were the linguistic and ethnic ancestors of the classical Greeks.

Ventris

Mycenaean Warfare

Some information about Mycenaean warfare was relayed through the epics of Homer, but philological and archaeological evidence from Greece, along with what is known from the Mycenaeans' contemporaries in Anatolia, Egypt, and the Levant, can go far in determining the nature of Mycenaean warfare.

Like their classical Greek descendants, the Mycenaeans appear to have possessed an aptitude for war that was eventually one of the factors in the demise of their society. For the most part, the Mycenaeans fought with weapons and methods similar to the Egyptians and Hittites; bronze swords and shields were used, along with chariots.

Linear B documents indicate that the Mycenaeans valued chariots as highly as their contemporaries, which is no surprise because chariots were the weapons and vehicles par excellence of most Bronze Age kingdoms, and the kingdoms that could afford to field armies with a sizable chariot corps, such as the Egyptians and Hittites, proved to be dominant. Most Bronze Age chariots were powered by two to four horses that carried teams of two to three men.

Hittite chariot teams consisted of three men: a driver, a shield bearer who protected the driver, and a warrior armed with a stabbing spear Macqueen 2003, 58). On the other hand, the Egyptians employed a two man chariot team: a driver, who doubled as an archer, and a shield bearer (Spalinger 2005, 18). It is unknown if the Mycenaeans employed two or three man chariot teams, but due to the simplicity and limitations of the design, it is safe to assume that they used one of the two methods. Extant Linear B documents from the Cretan city of Knossos depict chariots with and without wheels that were similar to chariots from other Bronze Age kingdoms (Chadwick 1973, 361-3).

One document in particular suggests that Mycenaean chariots were not only militarily functional, but also works of art. The tablet reads, "[Two] horse-(chariots without wheels) inlaid with ivory, (fully) assembled, painted crimson, equipped with bridles with leather check-straps (and) horn bits." (Chadwick 1973, 366).

Chariots are not the only Mycenaean weapons of war depicted in Linear B tablets; various forms of armor are also given attention. An ideogram in a number of Linear B tablets shows what appears to be a corselet, but whether they were made of bronze or thickly wadded linen is the subject of scholarly debates (Chadwick 1973, 375). Either possibility should be considered, though it is probable that Mycenaeans warriors wore both types of corselets depending on the warrior's status in society. Some Hittite warriors probably wore bronze corselets, and it is generally believed that higher ranking Egyptian chariot soldiers wore bronze (Spalinger 2005, 15).

Since charioteers were the elites of the Hittite and Egyptian armies, the same was probably true for the Mycenaeans. Thus, the Mycenaean charioteers probably wore bronze armor while most of the infantry was relegated to wearing linen armor. Archeological excavations from a warrior's grave at Knossos have revealed that Mycenaean warriors wore a number of different helmets. Many of the helmets discovered were made of bronze, while some were made of boar's tusk, which were probably only worn by nobles (Chadwick 1973, 376-7).

Ruth van Mierlo's picture of Mycenaean swords

Picture of a Mycenaean dagger

The Modern Discovery of Mycenaean Culture

The original source for all modern understanding of Mycenaean culture was the Greek poet Homer, and although some of the inherent problems of using the poet as a source have already been touched upon, more needs to be considered here. The subject matter of Homer's epics is clearly Mycenaean era Greece, but it cannot be stressed enough that his versions, which were culled from local traditions, were already hundreds of years old. In the period between the Trojan War and when Homer travelled around Greece reciting the story orally, there were countless opportunities for people to inject ideas and details into the stories. For instance, some sections obviously refer to Bronze Age Mycenaean traditions, such as the funeral games in Book 23, while other sections reflect the post-Mycenaean dark age Greece. The result is two epics that are at times anachronistic but for the most part reflective of many aspects of Mycenaean culture.

Although Homer's epics mostly belong in the category of fiction, they inspired one man to find the legendary city of Troy, which eventually paved the way for modern scholarship on Mycenaean culture. The scholar most intimately associated with the modern discovery of Troy and Mycenaean culture in general was the German businessman turned archeologist Heinrich Schliemann. As a boy, Schliemann became a Hellenophile as he read the Homeric epics and followed the Greek quest for independence closely (Chadwick 1973, 6). He also became an auto-didactic student of ancient history, consuming numerous books and learning ancient languages in his free time.

Schliemann

Despite his inherent love for all aspects of Greek culture, both ancient and modern, he travelled the world and amassed a small fortune through methods that some would consider unethical. For example, he cornered the saltpeter market during the Crimean War (1853-1856), bought gold off prospectors during the California gold rush, and finally speculated in cotton during the American Civil War (Wood 1985, 49). After his many financial ventures and adventures throughout the world, he retired from business and decided to dedicate the rest of his life to Greek archeology by moving his operations to Greece and Turkey and marrying a 16 year old Greek girl named Sophia (Chadwick 1973, 6).

Of course, Schliemann's primary task, and the one that would cement him in the annals of history, was locating and excavating the legendary city of Troy. Although Schliemann received no formal training in archeology, history, or philology, he eventually mastered a number of languages, and he knew how to use people who had formal training to his advantage. Perhaps delegating authority came naturally to Schliemann because of his business background, but whatever the case, it definitely proved to be successful in his archaeological endeavors.

Schliemann hired experienced archaeologists, such as Frank Calvert and Wilhelm Dörpfeld, to assist him and at times do much of the excavation work (Wood 1985, 55). He relied on his experienced and educated scholars to guide him in the direction where they thought the ruins of the legendary Troy were in what is now northwest Turkey, which is where he began preliminary excavations in 1870 (Wood 1985, 55). After three archaeological seasons, Schliemann was able to identify four strata (which were in effect different cities built atop the ruins of the previous ones) below the classical city of Ilium (Wood 1985, 57).

Calvert

Dörpfeld

It was not until the 1889-90 archaeological season that the remains of what was probably the legendary Troy were finally revealed. Dörpfeld found a number of Mycenaean pottery fragments and the remains of great towers, which all pointed to the ruins of the legendary Troy (later known as "Troy VI"). Today it is still not positively known if Troy VI or Troy VIIa was the Troy of the *Iliad*, but Schliemann and his band of 19th century archaeologists definitely found the correct location.

Perhaps more importantly than finding the location of the legendary Troy, Schliemann revealed the glories of Mycenaean culture to the modern world. As Schliemann assiduously worked to locate and unearth Troy, he was also involved in a number of excavations on mainland Greece. The most significant excavations he conducted in Greece were at the center of Mycenaean culture itself: Mycenae. Schliemann referred to the descriptions of the Greek geographer Pausanias to locate what he believed were the graves of Agamemnon and his companions, and at the site he discovered a bevy of intact jewels, which he named the "Jewels of Helen," and a number of gold face masks, one of which he believed was Agamemnon's funeral mask (Wood 1985, 68). Although it would later be revealed that the tomb and jewels he discovered at Mycenae predated Agamemnon and the Trojan War by three to four centuries, it was still one of the greatest archaeological discoveries of the modern world (Wood 1985, 70).

A picture of "Priam's Treasure," relics excavated by Schliemann's teams

A picture of Schliemann's wife wearing the "Jewels of Helen"

Schliemann essentially proved that the Trojan War did take place, although the scope of it was probably not what Homer claimed, and that there was a thriving culture on mainland Greece before the arrival of classical Greek culture. As a result, Schliemann's discoveries opened the door for modern scholars to enter the world of Mycenaean culture.

Mycenaean Trade and Contact with Other Peoples

During the height of their culture from about 1400-1200 BCE, the Mycenaeans were part of a complex trade network that connected the Aegean with the Levant, Egypt, and Anatolia, and the expansion of Mycenaean power is documented through texts, art, and archaeological remains. In particular, the Mycenaeans appear to have mastered the sea, much like their Aegean predecessors the Minoans, but ultimately the sea also played a major role in the collapse of the Mycenaean culture.

Before the Mycenaeans built complex trade networks that connected them to the likes of the Egyptians and Hittites, they developed land routes throughout Greece and into Europe. In fact, the Mycenaeans were the first people to bring roads to Europe, which they used to crisscross Greece for merchant activities (Samuel 1966, 103). Specifically, wheat from Thessaly and oil from Attica was imported to the primary Mycenaean cities of Mycenae, Pylos, and Tiryns on the Peloponnese (Samuel 1966, 103).

Eventually Mycenaean merchants penetrated deep into the Balkans region into what were non-Greek speaking areas, such as on the shores of Lake Ohrid in what is today modern Albania. Mycenaean pottery discovered in Albania testifies that Mycenaean trade goods, if not the Mycenaeans themselves, went to northern regions that classical Greeks knew little about hundreds of years later (Samuel 1966, 105). Mycenaean merchant activities in Greece and southeast Europe no doubt helped provide a template when the classical Greeks established more extensive and complex trade routes throughout the region 1,000 years later, despite the fact the Mycenaeans were basically forgotten until modern times.

The trade networks that the Mycenaeans established in southeast Europe were impressive, but the great wealth that was required to build the large tholos tombs discussed earlier was the result of extensive overseas trade with the long established kingdoms of the Bronze Age eastern Mediterranean. Although the Minoans are known for being a maritime power, the Mycenaeans eclipsed their Aegean neighbors when it came to open sea trade. The Mycenaeans were able to establish sea routes to the west long before the Minoans would attempt such a difficult journey, and they did so hundreds of years before the classical Greeks would exploit these very routes (Samuel 1966, 114). Specifically, the Mycenaeans established trade routes with the islands of Sardinia and Sicily, as well as the Libyan coastline (Morkot 1996, 28-29).

Archeological evidence seems to suggest that the Mycenaeans imported more goods than they exported; metal from Cyprus and Anatolia was imported to make weapons, while grain was imported from the Black Sea and Egypt (Vermeule 1960, 66). In return, the Mycenaeans exported their fine pottery and finished weapons throughout the Mediterranean (Morkot 1996, 28-29).

Picture of a Mycenaean vase in the Louvre

Picture of a Mycenaean gold earring in the Louvre

Trade obviously brought the Mycenaeans into direct contact with a number of different foreign peoples, especially the Egyptians and Hittites. Archeological evidence confirms that the Mycenaeans and the Egyptians had extensive contact with each other from about 1500-1300 BCE, but Egyptian-Aegean connections began long before that period; contact between the Egyptians and Minoans began before 2000 BCE, and from 2000-1500 BCE, permanent links between the two kingdoms appear to have been established. Egyptian scarabs and statues excavated at Knossos, dated to the Middle Minoan II period (ca. 2000-1700 BC), confirm contact between Egypt and the Aegean (Samuel 1966, 108).

The links that the Minoans established with Egypt were then taken over by the Mycenaeans around 1500 BCE, which coincided with the Late Helladic I period in Greece and when the first tholos tombs were built (Preziosi and Hitchcock 1999, 242). It is unknown in what context the Mycenaeans took over the role that the Minoans played in the Aegean-Egyptian trade network, but the evidence from Egypt is dated to the period right before the Mycenaeans conquered Crete, so it may have been a case of the Mycenaeans forcefully expanding their influence in the region and physically taking over the Minoan trade networks. Whatever the case, the first confirmed contact between the Mycenaeans and the Egyptians took place during the reign of the Egyptian king Thutmose III (ca. 1504-1450 BCE), who was known for his war-like nature and forceful expansion of the Egyptian empire. In that context, it may have been that the Egyptians sought the Mycenaeans out as partners to replace the increasingly weak Minoans.

A tomb of an Egyptian noble provides an interesting primary source on the relationship between the Mycenaeans and Egyptians during the Bronze Age. On the west bank of the Nile River across from the ancient city of Thebes are a collection of nobles' tombs, and most of the tombs are fairly standard in terms of New Kingdom design and function: they contain a sarcophagus that once housed the coffin and remains of the deceased. The walls of the tombs are adorned with formulaic inscriptions that were intended to help the deceased transition into the afterlife, but some of the inscriptions contain historical references that can help modern scholars reconstruct the nature of international relations during the Bronze Age.

The tomb of the vizier Rekhmire, who served under Thutmose III, is one of these tombs. Besides the numerous theological inscriptions and spells that comprise the majority of the texts in Rekhmire's tomb, there are some lines that refer to the "tribute" that the vizier oversaw coming into Egypt. The inscription reads, "Reception of the tribute of the south country, besides the tribute of Punt, the tribute of Retenu, the tribute of Keftyew, besides the booty of all countries which the fame of his majesty, King Menkheperre (Thutmose III) brought; by the heredity prince . . . Rekhmire." (Breasted 2001, 2:295-5). The peoples listed in the inscription are now identified as the following: Punt is the Horn of Africa (Faulkner 1999, 88); Retenu is Phoenicia/Lebanon (Faulkner 1999, 154); and Keftiyu is generally thought to refer to Crete (Faulkner 1999, 285).

Two important points are raised in this inscription concerning the nature of Mycenaean-Egyptian relations. If the Mycenaeans were trading partners with the Egyptians, why is Crete listed instead of mainland Greece, and why are they listed as giving tribute, which assumes an inferior status?

The first question can be answered by examining the relief that accompanies the text. In the relief, the Aegean ambassador is wearing a Mycenaean kilt, but closer examination reveals that the kilt was painted over traditional Minoan garb (Sandars 1987, 58). Apparently the Mycenaeans took over the Minoan-Egyptian trade network while Rekhmire was still alive, and the vizier then simply had the art in his tomb touched up to reflect the new trade partners.

The question of "tribute" is a bit more difficult to answer and probably concerns the Egyptians' image of themselves as much as semantics. The Egyptians viewed themselves as superior to all other peoples and depicted themselves as such in their art, especially during the New Kingdom, the period in which Rekhmire lived. Following this logic, foreign peoples, including the Mycenaeans, were never depicted as trading on an equal status with the Egyptians but were in an inferior position while bringing tribute to the Egyptians. The reality is the that Egyptian armies never came close to setting foot in Greece or even Crete, so the Egyptian text represents a propagandistic interpretation of reality. Moreover, the equivalent words for "trade" and "tribute" were essentially interchangeable in ancient Egyptian.

The high point of the Mycenaean-Egyptian trade network appears to have been during the reign of the Egyptian king Akhenaten (ca. 1364-1347 BC). It is during his reign that the highest volume of Mycenaean artifacts have been discovered in Egypt (Samuel 1966, 110).

The relationship between the Mycenaeans and Egyptians was fairly straightforward and reflected a relationship of reasonably equal status; but the relationship between the Mycenaeans and Hittites was more complex, and modern scholars are still searching to understand all its nuances. The Mycenaeans' relationship with the Hittites continues to be shrouded in mystery because scholars remain confused about where exactly the land the Hittites called "Ahhiyawa" was located. Many believe that Ahhiyawa was located on the western Anatolia coast or perhaps on the adjacent Aegean islands where some Mycenaean settlements were located (Kuhrt 2010, 1:237). The phonetic similarity between the word "Ahhiyawa" and "Achaean", which was the word used for many of the Mycenaeans by Homer, has led some to believe that they were one and the same (Bryce 2007, 57-60). Since the Mycenaeans were never unified under a central state and instead were a collection of several kingdoms, it may be that the Hittites referred to all Mycenaeans as "Ahhiyawa" without even knowing about mainland Greece (Samuel 1966, 126).

Other scholars, such as Eric Cline, have argued that Ahhiyawa referred to both the Mycenaeans as a people and mainland Greece geographically. Cline has further posited that the Mycenaeans are the only logical people who can be Ahhiyawa. He wrote, "However, we should not forget that there is, on the one hand, an important late bronze age culture otherwise unmentioned in the Hittite texts (Mycenaeans) and, on the other hand, an important textually attested late bronze age 'state' without archaeological remains (Ahhiyawa). It seems reasonable simply to equate the two." (Cline 1996, 145).

Archaeological and textual evidence from the ruins of the Hittite capital, Hattusa, give some more indications that the Mycenaeans were Ahhiyawa and their relationship with the Hittites was at times acrimonious. A Hittite letter dated to the reign of Tudhaliya II (ca. 1400-1390 BC) mentions that the Ahhiyawans may have been aligned with Aššura, which was an Anatolian state opposed to the Hittites (Cline 1996, 147). A fragment of a Hittite bowl discovered at Hattusa and dated to the late 15th century BCE depicts a warrior that looks remarkably similar to known images of Mycenaean warriors (Cline 1996, 147). A bronze sword was also discovered in the ruins of the Hittite capital in 1991 that was dated to the reign of Tudhaliya II and contains the following inscription: "As Duthaliya the Great King shattered the Aššuwas country, he dedicated these swords to the storm-god, his lord." (Cline 1996, 138). The sword is an interesting find because it is what archeologists term a Type B sword, which was indicative of Mycenaean workmanship.

The Hattusa sword and another similar one discovered near the modern Turkish city of Izmir represent another piece in the puzzle of Mycenaean-Hittite relations. The swords may have been brought from Greece by Mycenaean warriors who fought on the side of Aššura against the Hittites and left behind after battle, or, as the inscription on the Hattusa sword implies, they were spoils of war. The swords may also have been two of the many finished weapons that the Mycenaeans traded throughout the Mediterranean, or the swords may have been manufactured in Anatolia but inspired by the Mycenaean style (Cline 1996, 139).

Another Anatolian archaeological site, known as Panaztepe today, has also yielded remains of Mycenaean pottery, an Aegean sword, and Egyptian scarabs, which suggests that widespread international commerce may have taken place at the site (Cline 1996, 142). The totality of the sources clearly point to some interactions between the Mycenaean and Hittites, but the level and context of the contact remains open for debate.

Conversely, the extensive contact that the Mycenaeans had with the Minoans is unquestioned, and the latter obviously had immense influence over the culture of the former. As suggested earlier, the Mycenaeans had more in common with the Minoans than they did with later classical Greeks (despite sharing a similar language and ethnicity with them). While the Minoans were the preeminent culture in the Aegean, the Mycenaeans must have looked on the island people with a degree of admiration and possibly envy. Indeed, the Minoans represented the pinnacle of human civilization; they developed writing, created beautiful works of art, and developed long distance trade and communication with other civilizations.

Possibly out of a combination of this admiration and jealousy, the Mycenaeans conquered the Minoans sometime between 1450 and 1400 BCE, which was undoubtedly destructive but did not end the influence of Minoan culture in the Aegean. In fact, the Mycenaeans proved to be able bearers of Aegean civilization, just as the Romans were with Hellenic civilization when they conquered Greece around 1300 years later in 146 BCE.

The Mycenaeans' invention of Linear B script happened to coincide with their conquest of Crete, as did their role in the extensive international trade networks of the Late Bronze Age. In fact, the destruction that the Mycenaeans leveled on Crete when they invaded was for the most part minimal enough to allow them to quickly rebuild the primary city of Knossos so that it looked much as it did before they arrived (Preziosi and Hitchcock 1999, 167). An examination of the palace architecture and art at Knossos after the Mycenaean invasion reveals that any changes they made to the palace after they rebuilt it was done to meet their growing commercial needs (Preziosi and Hitchcock 1999, 165).

The largest and best documented Minoan palace is the one at Knossos, which was excavated and partly rebuilt by Arthur Evans. Evans discovered that what he called the New Palace at

Knossos was built over an earlier structure constructed in the third millennium B.C. The New Palace, built around 1700 B.C., was an elaborate structure that contained storerooms in the west wing and one of the most impressive spaces that Evans called the Throne Room.

The "Throne Room" of the Palace of Knossos

An entrance of four openings between piers leads down to an antechamber that was flanked by low benches. From this room one entered the Throne Rome, which had a stone throne placed against one long wall. It was surrounded by stone benches and faced a lustrum or ritual bathing chamber that was reached by a short staircase. The walls were decorated with frescoes with brightly painted griffins. While Evans thought that the throne he found was the earliest royal chair in Europe, it seems this ceremonial throne was more likely used by a priestess who sat among her colleagues and re-enacted the divine manifestation of the "Lady of the Labyrinth", the chief Minoan goddess.

Figurines of the Snake Goddess

To the south of the Throne Room was a chamber called the Snake Goddess Sanctuary, where Evans found a glazed earthenware image what he termed the Snake Goddess. Further on, the Temple of the Repositories yielded a number of images of the Snake Goddess that had been buried in the ground. Also in the west wing was the Cup Bearer Sanctuary, with frescoes of bearers of conical rhytons or ritual vessels used for offering liquid to the gods. A number of long narrow storerooms are also found in the west wing, apparently used to store tall pithoi (about 5 feet high earthenware vases with incised decorative patterns) that contained oil, wine and perhaps grain. Above these storage rooms was what Evans called the Great Sanctuary, which may have served as a venue for the public display of religious ceremonies.

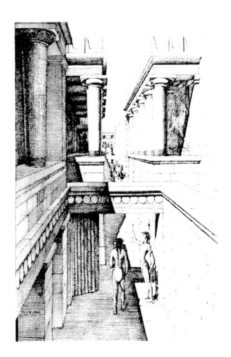

Evans' Reconstruction of Inner Gateway of the North Entrance of Palace at Knossos

One of the formal entrances to the Palace at Knossos was to the north. Beyond the entrance was the North Pillar Hall which may have served as a kind of anteroom or waiting room. It connected with the Bull Chamber, so named because it was decorated with a bull relief fresco.

The East Wing of the Palace contained workshops and a sanctuary of the Great Goddess on the second story that was accessed by means of a staircase from the central court. A grand staircase descended through two colonnaded landings down to the Hall of the Double Axes. Evans identified this area of the Palace as the Royal Apartments. Close by the Hall of the Double Axes is the Dolphin Sanctuary, so called because it contained a fresco showing bright blue Dolphins swimming in a sea surrounded by fish and sea urchins. Evans named this area of the palace the Queen's Apartment.

Dolphin fresco

The palace of Knossos is known as much for its beautiful frescoes as it is for its expansive palace, and after the Mycenaeans conquered Crete, they continued to employ many of the Minoan artistic traditions, which continue to capture the imagination of modern people. Perhaps the best known and most beautifully rendered of the wall frescoes that adorned the palace at Knossos are the scenes that depict young men leaping over bulls. People of many different cultures throughout several different periods of time have associated bulls with symbols of strength and fertility (Kyle 2007, 41). The ancient Egyptians worshipped a living bull, known as the Apis, because they believed it was associated with the god of the dead, Osiris. The Egyptians also venerated the Apis for its potency (Shaw and Nicholson 1995, 35-36).

It appears that the Minoans and the Mycenaeans also may have valued bulls for their strength and vitality and thus engaged in these events; but many questions remain concerning their details. It is unknown if the participants in the bull leaping events were voluntary elites, impetuous young men, or slaves forced to compete against their will (Kyle 2007, 42). The purpose of the bull leaping events is also unknown; some suggest that it was an annual coming-of-age ritual (Kyle 2007, 43), while others believe that it was a ritualized reenactment of early bovine domestication (Preziosi and Hitchcock 1999, 169).

Svilen Enev's picture of a silver rhyton (circa 1600 BCE) found in Mycenae

A bull leaping fresco found in Knossos

Whatever the purpose, most scholars believe that these were real events, and some think that the Mycenaeans later imported the events to mainland Greece. A fresco dated from around the time the Mycenaeans conquered Crete (ca. 1450 BCE) discovered at Mycenae depicts both males and females leaping over bulls as female spectators watch on from a window (Kyle 2007, 44). Frescoes from Tiryns and Pylos, dated to the 13th century BCE, also depict males and females competing in bull leaping events, which suggests that either the Mycenaeans imported the idea to mainland Greece after they conquered Crete and learned of the events, or that they had already competed in the events but imported the artistic idea of depicting them in frescoes after the conquest.

Whoever the competitors were, and whatever the purpose of the Minoan bull leaping events, it is evident that the Mycenaeans also competed in these events, and they were obviously important to both Aegean peoples.

The Trojan War

Mycenaean influence in the Mediterranean reached its zenith around the time of the legendary Trojan War, during which perhaps thousands of Mycenaean warriors converged on the Anatolian city and then dispersed after its destruction to invoke the same fate on numerous other cities, some of them Mycenaean.

The historicity of the Trojan War is no longer debated, but scholars still argue over its scope, and, by extension, its overall impact on Mycenaean culture and the Late Bronze Age in general. To begin with, establishing a date for the war is important in terms of the overall historical context. Numerous classical historians place the destruction of Troy sometime between 1334 and 1183 BCE (Wood 1985, 28), while some modern scholars assign a more precise date of 1220 BCE (Drews 1993, 42). This date for the destruction of Troy is based on the more general movements and destructions caused by the various peoples generally referred to as the "Sea Peoples" (which will be discussed further below). On this matter, it is important to note that the Greeks of Homer's epics, including Agamemnon, the king of Mycenae, did not call themselves Mycenaeans or even Greeks but Achaeans, Danaans, or Argives (Wood 1985, 21).

One of the more interesting accounts of the Trojan War comes from Herodotus' *Histories*. The Greek historian related an Egyptian version of the Trojan War that emphasized the importance of Egypt and the Egyptians in the war's aftermath:

> I asked the priests if the Greek story of what happened at Troy had any truth in it, and they gave me in reply some information which they claimed to have had direct from Menelaus himself. This was, that after the abduction of Helen, the Greeks sent a strong force to the Troad in support of Menelaus' cause, and as soon as the men had landed and established themselves on Trojan soil, ambassadors, of whom Menelaus was one, were dispatched to Troy. They were received within the walls of the town, and demanded the restoration of Helen together with the treasure which Paris had stolen, and also satisfaction for the injuries they had received. The Trojans, however, gave them the answer which they always stuck to afterwards – sometimes even swearing to the truth of it: namely, that neither Helen nor the treasure was in their possession, but both were in Egypt, and there was no justice in trying to force them to give satisfaction for property which was being detained by the Egyptian king Proteus. The Greeks, supposing this to be a merely frivolous answer, laid siege to the town, and persisted until it fell; but no Helen was found, and they were still told the same story, until at last they believed it and sent Menelaus to visit Proteus in Egypt. He sailed up river to Memphis, and when he had given a true account of all that had happened, he was most hospitably entertained and Helen, having suffered no evils, was restored to him with all the rest of his property. Nevertheless, in spite of this generous treatment, Menelaus proved himself no friend to Egypt; for when he wished to leave, but was delayed for a long time by contrary winds, he took two Egyptian children and offered them in sacrifice. The discovery of this foul act turned the friendship of the Egyptians to hatred; he was pursued, but managed to escape with his ships to Libya. Where he went afterwards the Egyptians could not say. They told me that they had learned of some of these events by inquiry, but spoke with certain knowledge of those which had taken place in their own country." (Herodotus, The Histories, II, 118-19).

It is believed that Herodotus did not question the historicity of the Trojan War, but only whether the Egyptians had their own version of it, which they apparently did (Wood 1985, 27). Much of Herodotus' work is based on oral testimony, so it follows that he would have searched for alternative oral traditions of the Trojan War. It is also noteworthy that by the time Herodotus compiled his work in the 5th century BCE, more than one version of the Trojan War existed that catered to specific ethnic groups. It was in a similar cultural milieu that the 1st century BCE Roman poet Virgil penned his *Aeneid*, which ascribed the origins of the Romans to Troy.

Troy and the Trojan War obviously continued to inspire the imaginations of Greeks and non-Greeks alike for centuries, and the fact that most ancient knowledge of the war was based on the semi-fictional accounts of Homer was not a problem for the ancients. Today, the line between myth and reality is clearly delineated in the minds of most, but 2,000 years ago, people were more apt to blur those lines, especially when it came to the Trojan War. Strabo perhaps best describes how the ancients resolved this dichotomy as it related to Homer. The geographer wrote:

> "Just so was Homer wont to add a mythical element to actual occurrences, thus giving flavour and adornment to his style; but he as the same end in view as the historian or the person who narrates facts. So, for instance, he took the Trojan war, an historical fact, and decked it out with his myths; and he did the same in the case of the wanderings of Odysseus; but to hand an empty story of marvels on something wholly untrue is not Homer's way of doing things. For it occurs to us at once, doubtless, that a man will lie more plausibly if he will mix in some actual truth, just as Polybius says, when his is discussing the wanderings of Odysseus. This is what Homer himself means when he says of Odysseus: 'So he told many lies in the likeness of truth;' for Homer does not say 'all' but 'many' lies; since otherwise they would not have been 'in the likeness of truth.' Accordingly, he took the foundations of his stories from history." (Strabo, Geography, 1, II.9).

This interesting passage elucidates how important the Trojan War continued to be in the minds of the Greeks and Romans, and how they were willing to absolve the apparent conflict between history and myth, which to the modern mind seems inconceivable.

Although the Trojan War influenced people's imaginations for centuries afterwards, its true extent is still unknown, and the debate over whether the ruins of Troy VI or VIIa represent the city of the Trojan War continues. Many, including Schliemann and Dörpfeld, believed that Troy VI most closely resembled Homer's description of the city due to the ruins of large walls excavated at that level, but its destruction came around 1300 BC, which is considered by some to be too early to be the legendary city (Morkot 1996, 35). It is also likely that Troy VI suffered from a major earthquake, which may have been the ultimate cause of that city's collapse (Drews 1993, 37).

The remains of Troy VIIa show it to have been a much poorer city materially speaking, which is an argument against it being the Troy of Homer's epics, but its destruction is much closer to the date of 1220 BCE that modern scholars ascribe to the more widespread man-made destruction of war. Although little Mycenaean pottery was found at the Troy VIIa level, it is entirely possible that both destructions were man-made and caused by the Mycenaeans (Drews 1993, 41-42).

The Collapse of the Mycenaean Culture

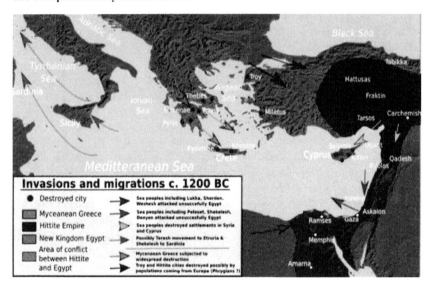

A map indicating the collapse of the Bronze Age due to foreign invasions

Ironically, modern scholars now believe that regardless of whether it was the legendary city of Troy from the *Iliad*, the destruction of Troy VIIa was committed by the Sea Peoples, and that it also signaled the beginning of the end of Mycenaean culture. (Vermeule 1960, 66).

Beginning around 1220 BCE, the Bronze Age system that the Mycenaeans were a part of came crashing down in a series of raids, invasions, and sackings by a mysterious collection of disparate peoples now known collectively as the Sea Peoples. The Sea Peoples contributed to the destruction of the Hittite Empire and the kingdom of Ugarit, and they even unsuccessfully attacked Egypt twice.

The Sea Peoples invasions were also a major factor in the collapse of the Mycenaean culture, which is ironic since at least some of the Sea Peoples tribes were ethnic Mycenaeans. The Sea Peoples were a number of different tribes who only occasionally seemed to have worked together, and they were mostly illiterate, so all modern information about them and their movements comes through archeology, classical Greek and Roman sources that were written hundreds of years later, and (most importantly) ancient Egyptian inscriptions. The Egyptians successfully repulsed two attacks by Sea Peoples confederations around 1219 BCE during the reign of Merenptah and around 1162 BCE during the rule of Ramesses III. Both of these wars were commemorated by the Egyptians on the walls of their temples in both hieroglyphic inscriptions and pictorial reliefs, which have provided modern scholars with the most information about the Sea Peoples in terms of the names of their tribes, what type of clothing they wore, and what type of weapons they used.

The inscriptions concerning the first Sea Peoples attack on Egypt relates important information about the Mycenaean-Sea Peoples connection. According to the Egyptian sources, a battle between the Egyptian army led by the pharaoh Merenptah and a Sea Peoples confederation of five tribes allied with the Libyans took place that lasted for six hours and left 9,000 Sea Peoples and Libyans dead (Breasted 2001, 3:239). The names of the five tribes are enumerated in the inscriptions: "The wretched, fallen chief of Libya, Meryey, son of Ded, has fallen upon the country of Tehenu with his bowmen . . . Sherden, Shekelesh, Ekwesh, Luka, Teresh, taking the best of every warrior and every man of war of his country. He has brought his wife and his children . . . leaders of the camp, and he has reached the western boundary in the fields of Perire." (Breasted, 2001, 243).

Unlike the Sea Peoples attack on Egypt during the reign of Merenptah, the attack during Ramesses III came from the northeast, and this time the invaders apparently planned to stay because the pictorial representations depict the invaders being followed by women, children, and farm animals (Cline 2003, 117). The Libyans were absent in the second attack, but the Shardana were there along with five new tribes. The inscription reads, "The countries . . . the [Northerners] in their isles were disturbed, taken away in the fray . . . at one time. Not one stood before their hands, from Kheta, Kode, Carchemish, Arvad, Alasa, they were wasted. [The]y [set up] a camp in one place in Amor. They desolated his people and his land like that which is not. They came with fire prepared before them, forward to Egypt. Their main support was Peleset, Thekel, Shekelesh, Denyen, and Weshesh, (these) lands were united, and they laid their hands upon the land as far as the Circle of the Earth. Their hearts confident, full of their plans." (Breasted 2001, 37-38).

Of all the Sea Peoples tribes enumerated in the Egyptian inscriptions, modern scholars have identified two as being Mycenaeans/Greeks and possibly one as Trojan. The Greeks of the Homeric epics were referred to as Achaeans, Danaans, or Argives, but never as Mycenaeans or Greeks, so some scholars believe that the "Denyen" mentioned in the inscriptions of Ramesses III were a Mycenaean tribe, while the Teresh listed in the documents from the reign of Merenptah were remnants from Troy (Vermeule 1960, 67).

The linguistic similarities between the names is about the only evidence that currently exists for the identification of the Denyen with Mycenaeans and the Teresh with Trojans, but identifying the Ekwesh (who were part of the first attack on Egypt) with the Achaeans/Mycenaeans may be more convincing. The phonetic similarity between "Ekwesh" and "Achaean" is the first argument to be made in favor of assigning the Mycenaeans to the roster of this tribe of Sea Peoples. The word "Ekwesh" may have been the Egyptians' attempt to reproduce the word "Achoioi", which was actually the ancient Greek world for "Achaean" (Cline 2003, 114).

For more corroborating evidence, scholars have turned to Homer. One passage from The Odyssey in particular seems to not only corroborate the historicity of the Trojan War but also the identification of the Achaeans with the Ekwesh. The passage reads:

"So for nine years we Achaeans campaigned at Troy; and after sacking Priam's city in the tenth we sailed for home and our fleet was scattered by a god. But for my unhappy self the inventive brain of Zeus was hatching more mischief. I had spent only a month in the delights of home life with my children, my wife and my possessions, when the spirit moved me to fit out some ships and sail for Egypt with heroic companions. I got nine vessels ready and the crews were soon mustered . . .Then I ordered my good men to stay by the ships on guard while I sent out some scouts to reconnoiter from the heights. But, carried away by their own violence they went on a rampage, and immediately began to plunder some of the fine Egyptian farms, carrying off the women and children and killing the men. The hue and cry soon reached the city, and the townsfolk, roused by the alarm, poured out at dawn. The whole place was filled with infantry and chariots and glint of arms. Zeus the Thunderer struck abject panic into my party. Not a man had the spirit to stand and face the enemy, for we were threatened on all sides. They ended by cutting down a large part of my force with their sharp weapons and carrying off the survivors to work for them as slaves." (Homer, The Odyssey, XIV, 240-270).

When considered along with the Egyptian sources, a potential course of events can be reconstructed as follows: Odysseus and his Achaeans/Mycenaeans left Greece around 1230 BCE to lay siege to Troy, and after sacking the city 10 years later, they sailed south to Egypt, where they allied with the Libyans and four other tribes but were repulsed by the Egyptians.

Based on this, the Ekwesh were Mycenaeans, but this immediately raises the question of why the Mycenaeans would be one of the tribes of Sea Peoples when other Sea Peoples were essentially destroying the Mycenaean culture? The answer to that question is difficult to answer and probably involves several different factors, but land pressure from the north, in the form of migrating/invading peoples, may have caused a domino effect that forced some of the Achaeans/Mycenaeans to become the Ekwesh Sea People (Vermeule 1960, 68).

While the Sea Peoples were ravaging the coastlines of the eastern Mediterranean, a new group of people called the Dorians entered Greece by land from the north. The Dorians were illiterate Greek speaking people, and they were quite backwards compared to the Mycenaeans, but they were able to use the instability and anarchy to their advantage (Vermeule 1960, 66). The Dorians eventually worked their way south, marauding as they went, until they had enveloped the Peloponnese and even Crete between 1100 and 950 BCE (Vermeule 1960, 66). Although the Dorians adopted some aspects of Mycenaean culture, and along with the Mycenaeans were the linguistic and ethnic ancestors of the classical Greeks, they essentially represented the end of the Mycenaean age.

Given the uncertainty regarding the chronology of events, it's unclear whether the Mycenaean cities were the victims of destructive invasions or whether their decline was just a consequence of those events elsewhere. Although the Sea Peoples and Dorians caused widespread destruction to the major Mycenaean population centers (Morkot 1996, 33), Vermeule convincingly argued that it was the disruption of the trade networks caused by the invasions, not the invasions themselves, which ultimately led to the collapse of the Mycenaean culture. As discussed earlier, the Mycenaeans imported large amounts of grain and metal from abroad to feed their population and arm their armies, so any disruption of these routes may have resulted in a severe crisis worse than anything a few sieges of cities could have done (Vermeule 1960, 66-67). If the grain shipments from Egypt and the Black Sea region were reduced, or even stopped completely, then the large population centers of Mycenae, Pylos, and Tiryns would have suffered famine and eventually population loss. Also, the lack of metals imported to Greece would have resulted in fewer weapons for the Mycenaean armies, which, combined with the lowered and weakened population from famine, would have meant that the primary population centers would have been less protected. Not many raids would have been needed to precipitate such a situation as its effects would have snowballed, and the Mycenaeans, who had no central government (unlike the Hittites and Egyptians), would have been particularly susceptible to such a situation, as many young Mycenaean warriors would have then decided to join the ranks of the Sea Peoples in order to survive and thrive (Vermeule 1960, 71).

Some of the stronger Mycenaean kingdoms may have seen the writing on the wall and tried to hold the trade networks together forcefully, which may have been the true cause of the Trojan War (Redford 1992, 253). The various independent Mycenaean kingdoms from the mainland may have formed a confederacy to hold on to control of the northern trade routes that connected their cities to the Hittites, but even in victory, the Mycenaeans seem to have been their own worst enemies because a number of them broke from the main body and became the Ekwesh. In other words, it was not the Mycenaeans who disappeared but their culture.

As part of a larger Aegean civilization, the Mycenaeans were heavily dependent to some extent on Crete, Hatti, and Egypt for ideas and trade, but when those lines were cut, Aegean civilization collapsed and Greece regressed into a dark age (Vermeule 1960, 74). The Greek dark age lasted for about 300 years, but when the new Hellenic civilization emerged in the 8th century, it was indebted to the Mycenaeans in a number of intangible ways. Although the Greeks learned writing from the Phoenicians, their language came from the Mycenaeans, and no doubt their love for war did as well. Mycenaean religion also apparently carried over to the classical period to a certain extent, especially the worship of Zeus and Poseidon who were two of the most important deities in the classical Greek pantheon.

Perhaps one of the most important traits that the Mycenaeans passed on to the classical Greeks was the spirit of travel and adventure. The trade routes that the Mycenaeans established in the 15th century BCE were duplicated and expanded upon centuries later when the Greeks built colonies and trading ports in Sicily, Libya, Egypt, and along the coast of the Black Sea.

Of course, the most enduring legacy that the Mycenaeans left for the Greeks and the rest of the world consist of the oral traditions that Homer turned into masterpieces centuries later. After Homer turned the brave deeds of Mycenaean warriors into poems and prose, legions of students of the Greek language have been introduced to the Mycenaean world, which is a world that will no doubt continue to be explored through the methods of modern archaeology.

Online Resources

Other books about ancient history by Charles River Editors

Other books about Ancient Greece on Amazon

Bibliography

Arrian. 1971. *The Campaigns of Alexander.* Translated by Aubrey de Sélincourt. London: Penguin Books.

Bagnall, Nigel. 2002. *The Punic Wars: 246-146 BC*. London: Osprey Publishing.

Berlin, Andrea M. 1997. "From Monarchy to Markets: The Phoenicians in Hellenistic Palestine." *Bulletin of the American Schools of Oriental Research* 306: 75-88.

Bikai, Patricia Maynor. 1989. "Cyprus and the Phoenicians." *Biblical Archaeologist* 52: 203 209.

Breasted, James Henry, ed. and trans. 2001. *Ancient Records of Egypt*. Vol. 2, *The Eighteenth Dynasty*. Chicago: University of Illinois Press.

Cochavi-Rainey, Zipora, trans and ed. 1999. *Royal Gifts in the Late Bronze Age Fourteenth to Thirteenth Centuries BCEE.: Selected Texts Recording Gifts to Royal Personages.* Jerusalem: Ben-Gurion University of the Negev Press.

Crawford, Michael. 2001. "Early Rome and Italy." In *The Oxford history of the Roman world*, ed. John Boardman, Jasper Griffin, and Oswyn Murray, 50-73. Oxford: Oxford University Press.

Diodorus. 2004. *The Library of History.* Translated by C.H. Oldfather. Cambridge, Massachusetts: Harvard University Press.

Herm, Gerhard. 1975. *The Phoenicians: The Purple Empire of the Ancient Near East.* Translated   by Caroline Hillier. New York: William Morrow and Company.

Herodotus. 2003. *The Histories.* Translated by Aubrey de Sélincourt. London: Penguin Books.

Kuhrt, Amélie. 2010. *The Ancient Near East: c. 3000-330 BC.* 2 vols. London: Routledge.

Lichtheim, Miriam, ed. 1976. *Ancient Egyptian Literature.* Vol. 2, *The New Kingdom.* Los Angeles: University of California Press.

Livy. 1996. *The War with Hannibal.* Translated by Aubrey de Sélincourt. London: Penguin Books.

Lloyd, Alan B. 1975. "Were Necho's Triremes Phoenician?" *Journal of Hellenic Studies* 95: 45-   61.

Lucas, A. and J.R. Harris. 1999. *Ancient Egyptian Materials and Industries.* Mineola, New York: Dover Publications.

Luckenbill, Daniel David, trans. and ed. 1989. *Ancient Records of Assyria and Babylonia.* 2 vols.   London: Histories and Mysteries of Man.

Markoe, Glenn E. 2000. *Phoenicians.* Los Angeles: University of California Press.

Moran, William L. ed. and trans. 1992. *The Amarna Letters.* Baltimore: John Hopkins University   Press.

Morkot, Robert. 1996. *The Penguin Historical Atlas of Ancient Greece.* London: Penguin Books.

Moscati, Sabatino. 1968. *The World of the Phoenicians.* Translated by Alastair Hamilton. New York: Frederick A. Praeger.

Noureddine, Ibrahim. 2010. "New Light on the Phoenician Harbor at Tyre." *Near Eastern Archaeology* 73: 176-181.

Pritchard, James B, ed. 1992. *Ancient Near Eastern Texts Relating to the Old Testament.* 3rd ed. Princeton, New Jersey: Princeton University Press.

Scarre, Chris. 1995. *The Penguin Historical Atlas of Ancient Rome*. London: Penguin Books.

Stern, E. 1990. "New Evidence from Dor for the First Appearance of the Phoenicians along the Northern Coast of Israel." *Bulletin of the American Schools of Oriental Research* 279: 27-34.

Strabo. 2001. *Geography*. Translated by Horace Leonard Jones. Cambridge, Massachusetts: Harvard University Press.

Watson-Treumann, Brigette. 2001. "Beyond the Cedars of Lebanon: Phoenician Timber Merchants and Trees from the 'Black Mountain.'" *Die Welt des Orients* 31: 75-83.

Wright, Edmund, ed. 2006. *A Dictionary of World History*. 2nd ed. Oxford: Oxford University Press.

Xenophon. 1972. *The Persian Expedition*. Translated by Rex Warner. London: Penguin Books.

Free Books by Charles River Editors

We have brand new titles available for free most days of the week. To see which of our titles are currently free, click on this link.

Discounted Books by Charles River Editors

We have titles at a discount price of just 99 cents everyday. To see which of our titles are currently 99 cents, click on this link.

Printed in Great Britain
by Amazon